A Happiness Self Help Book

Crafted by Skriuwer

Table of Contents

6. **Introduction**
- Definition and importance of happiness
- Overview of the book's approach and goals
- Structure and key components of the book
- Practical tips for applying the content

15. **Chapter 1: Understanding Happiness**
- What is happiness? Various definitions and perspectives
- The difference between happiness and pleasure
- Psychological and biological aspects of happiness
- Key theories and models
- How different cultures view and pursue happiness
- Historical shifts in the concept of happiness

26. **Chapter 2: Self-Awareness and Personal Growth**
- Techniques for understanding your values, strengths, and passions
- The role of self-awareness in happiness
- The importance of being true to yourself
- Strategies for cultivating authenticity in daily life
- How goal-setting contributes to happiness
- SMART goals and actionable steps for achieving personal goals

37. **Chapter 3: Building Positive Relationships**
- The impact of relationships on happiness
- Understanding the quality vs. quantity of relationships
- Techniques for improving communication with others
- Active listening and empathetic responses
- The importance of forgiveness for personal happiness
- Strategies for resolving conflicts and maintaining healthy relationships

| 48. | **Chapter 4: Mindfulness and Emotional Well-being** |

- What is mindfulness and how it contributes to happiness
- Techniques for incorporating mindfulness into daily life
- Understanding the impact of stress on happiness
- Tools and strategies for stress management
- The benefits of practicing gratitude
- Methods for incorporating gratitude into your routine

| 59. | **Chapter 5: Healthy Lifestyle Choices** |

- How physical health impacts mental well-being
- Creating a balanced lifestyle with diet, exercise, and sleep
- The role of physical activity in boosting happiness
- Finding enjoyable forms of exercise
- The impact of diet on mood and energy levels
- Tips for a nutritious and balanced diet

| 71. | **Chapter 6: Finding Purpose and Meaning** |

- Exploring what gives your life meaning and fulfillment
- Techniques for identifying and pursuing your purpose
- The happiness benefits of giving and helping others
- Opportunities for volunteer work and community involvement
- Finding satisfaction in your career or academic pursuits
- Strategies for aligning your work with your passions and values

| 83. | **Chapter 7: Overcoming Challenges and Adversity** |

- Developing resilience in the face of adversity
- Techniques for coping with challenges and setbacks
- The role of adaptability in maintaining happiness
- Strategies for embracing and managing change
- Understanding and managing negative emotions
- Tools for transforming negative feelings into positive growth

96. Chapter 8: Creating a Joyful Environment
- How your physical environment affects your mood
- Tips for creating a positive and uplifting living space
- Techniques for maintaining a positive outlook
- The role of optimism in achieving happiness
- Identifying and pursuing activities that bring joy and fulfillment
- Balancing work and leisure for a happier life

109. Chapter 9: Sustaining Happiness Over Time
- The role of habits in maintaining happiness
- Strategies for creating and sustaining positive habits
- Importance of periodic self-assessment and reflection
- Adjusting your goals and strategies for continuous improvement
- Recognizing and celebrating your successes and milestones
- The impact of celebration on overall happiness

120. Conclusion
- Recap of the main strategies and insights for achieving happiness
- Motivational message to inspire continued pursuit of happiness
- Next Steps and Continued Learning

126. Appendices
- Self-Assessment Tools
- Resource List
- Gratitude Journal Template

Introduction

Definition and Importance of Happiness

Happiness is a complex and multidimensional emotional state that is characterized by feelings of joy, contentment, and overall well-being. It is a fundamental aspect of human experience and plays a crucial role in shaping our quality of life and overall satisfaction. While happiness is subjective and can vary from person to person, it is generally considered a positive and desirable state of being that is essential for leading a fulfilling and meaningful life.

Importance of Happiness:

1. Psychological Well-being: Happiness is closely linked to mental health and psychological well-being. Research has shown that individuals who experience higher levels of happiness are less likely to suffer from mental health issues such as depression and anxiety. Cultivating a sense of happiness can improve overall emotional resilience and coping mechanisms.

2. Physical Health: The benefits of happiness extend beyond mental well-being to physical health. Studies have indicated that happy individuals tend to have lower levels of stress hormones, reduced inflammation, and better cardiovascular health. Positive emotions can boost the immune system and contribute to overall longevity.

3. Relationships: Happiness plays a crucial role in fostering positive relationships with others. Happy individuals are more likely to engage in pro-social behaviors, exhibit empathy and compassion, and form strong and lasting connections with friends, family, and colleagues. Cultivating happiness can enhance the quality of our relationships and social interactions.

4. Productivity and Success: A happy and fulfilled individual is more likely to be motivated, creative, and productive in their personal and professional endeavors. Happiness can enhance performance, decision-making, and problem-solving skills, leading to greater success and fulfillment in various aspects of life.

5. Resilience and Coping: Happiness acts as a buffer against adversity and challenges. Individuals who experience higher levels of happiness are better equipped to cope with stress, setbacks, and life's uncertainties. Cultivating happiness can enhance resilience, adaptability, and the ability to bounce back from difficult situations.

6. Quality of Life: Ultimately, happiness is a key determinant of our overall quality of life. It influences our perceptions, attitudes, and behaviors, shaping our experiences and interactions with the world around us. By prioritizing happiness and well-being, individuals can enhance their overall life satisfaction and sense of fulfillment.

In conclusion, happiness is a vital aspect of human existence that contributes to our overall well-being, health, relationships, and success. Understanding the definition and importance of happiness can serve as a foundation for embarking on a journey towards a joyful and fulfilling life. By cultivating happiness through self-awareness, positive relationships, mindfulness, healthy lifestyle choices, purpose-driven actions, resilience, and a positive environment, individuals can enhance their overall happiness and well-being for sustained fulfillment and personal growth.

Overview of the book's approach and goals

A Happiness Self Help Book is a carefully crafted guide designed to help individuals navigate the complexities of achieving true happiness and fulfillment in their lives. This book takes a holistic approach to happiness, addressing various aspects of life that contribute to overall well-being. In this section, we will delve into the overview of the book's approach and goals, providing insight into the key themes and objectives that underpin its content.

Approach:
The book takes a multi-faceted approach to happiness, recognizing that true joy and fulfillment come from a combination of factors such as self-awareness, positive relationships, mindfulness, healthy lifestyle choices, finding purpose and meaning, overcoming challenges, creating a joyful environment, and sustaining happiness over time. By exploring these different dimensions of happiness, the book aims to provide readers with a comprehensive toolkit for cultivating a more meaningful and joyful existence.

Goals:
The primary goal of A Happiness Self Help Book is to empower readers to take proactive steps towards enhancing their overall well-being and leading a more fulfilling life. Through practical tips, evidence-based strategies, and insightful reflections, the book aims to guide individuals on a journey of self-discovery and personal growth. By fostering a deeper understanding of happiness and the key components that contribute to it, the book seeks to inspire readers to make positive changes in their lives and embrace a more positive and purposeful way of living.

Specific goals outlined in the book include:

1. Understanding Happiness: By exploring the concept of happiness from various perspectives and shedding light on its psychological, biological, and cultural dimensions, the book aims to help readers develop a deeper understanding of what happiness truly means and how it can be attained.

2. Cultivating Self-Awareness and Personal Growth: Through techniques for self-discovery, goal-setting, and authenticity, the book encourages readers to tap into their inner strengths and passions, fostering personal growth and a sense of purpose.

3. Building Positive Relationships: Recognizing the profound impact of relationships on happiness, the book provides guidance on improving communication, practicing forgiveness, and resolving conflicts, in order to cultivate healthy and fulfilling connections with others.

4. Promoting Mindfulness and Emotional Well-being: By introducing mindfulness practices, stress management tools, and gratitude exercises, the book aims to help readers enhance their emotional well-being and develop a more positive outlook on life.

5. Encouraging Healthy Lifestyle Choices: Through insights on the connection between physical health and mental well-being, the book advocates for a balanced lifestyle that includes proper nutrition, regular exercise, and sufficient sleep, to support overall happiness and vitality.

6. Finding Purpose and Meaning: By guiding readers in exploring their passions, values, and life purpose, the book encourages individuals to seek fulfillment through meaningful activities, volunteer work, and alignment of their work with their personal values.

7. Building Resilience and Overcoming Adversity: Offering strategies for coping with challenges, managing negative emotions, and embracing change, the book aims to help readers develop resilience and adaptability in the face of adversity, fostering a sense of inner strength and perseverance.

8. Creating a Joyful Environment: By emphasizing the importance of a positive physical environment, optimism, and engaging in activities that bring joy, the book seeks to inspire readers to cultivate a space that nurtures happiness and fosters a sense of well-being.

9. Sustaining Happiness Over Time: Through insights on habit formation, self-assessment, goal adjustment, and celebration of achievements, the book aims to support readers in maintaining long-term happiness and continuous personal growth.

Overall, A Happiness Self Help Book serves as a comprehensive roadmap for individuals seeking to embark on a journey towards a more joyful and fulfilling life. By integrating practical tips, evidence-based strategies, and insightful reflections, the book empowers readers to take charge of their happiness and create a life filled with purpose, meaning, and contentment.

Structure and key components of the book

The book "A Happiness Self Help Book" offers a thorough exploration of various aspects that contribute to living a happy and fulfilling life. The structure and key components of the book provide a roadmap for readers to navigate their journey towards happiness.

The book is divided into nine chapters, each focusing on a specific aspect of happiness and personal development.

In the Introduction, the author sets the stage by defining happiness and emphasizing its importance in leading a fulfilling life. The overview of the book's approach and goals is outlined to give readers a glimpse of what to expect. This section also provides practical tips for applying the content discussed throughout the book.

Chapter 1 delves into the fundamental concept of happiness, exploring various definitions and perspectives. It distinguishes between happiness and pleasure and discusses the psychological and biological aspects of happiness. Key theories and models such as Positive Psychology and Hedonic Adaptation are introduced, along with insights into how different cultures view and pursue happiness and historical shifts in the concept of happiness.

Chapter 2 focuses on self-awareness and personal growth, highlighting the significance of understanding one's values, strengths, and passions. It underscores the role of self-awareness in happiness and provides strategies for cultivating authenticity in daily life. The chapter also delves into the importance of goal-setting and offers actionable steps for achieving personal goals using the SMART framework.

Building positive relationships is the central theme of Chapter 3, emphasizing the impact of relationships on happiness. It explores the quality versus quantity of relationships, communication techniques, active listening, empathy, forgiveness, conflict resolution, and maintaining healthy relationships.

Chapter 4 shifts the focus to mindfulness and emotional well-being, explaining how mindfulness contributes to happiness and offering techniques for incorporating mindfulness into daily life. Stress management tools, the benefits of gratitude practice, and methods for integrating gratitude into one's routine are also discussed.

Healthy lifestyle choices are explored in Chapter 5, highlighting the connection between physical health and mental well-being. The chapter emphasizes the importance of a balanced lifestyle encompassing diet, exercise, and sleep, and provides tips for finding enjoyable forms of exercise and maintaining a nutritious diet.

Finding purpose and meaning in life is the central theme of Chapter 6, guiding readers through techniques for identifying and pursuing their purpose. The chapter also explores the happiness benefits of giving back, volunteer work, community involvement, and aligning one's work with passions and values.

Chapter 7 addresses overcoming challenges and adversity, focusing on developing resilience, coping strategies, adaptability, managing change, understanding and transforming negative emotions, and fostering personal growth in the face of setbacks.

Creating a joyful environment is the focus of Chapter 8, exploring how the physical environment influences mood and offering tips for creating a positive living space. The chapter also emphasizes the role of optimism, pursuing activities that bring joy, and balancing work and leisure for a happier life.

In Chapter 9, sustaining happiness over time is discussed, highlighting the role of habits in maintaining happiness, strategies for creating positive habits, self-assessment, reflection, continuous improvement, and celebrating successes and milestones.

The book concludes by summarizing the main strategies and insights for achieving happiness, providing a motivational message to inspire continued pursuit of happiness, and offering suggestions for further reading and resources. Appendices include self-assessment tools, a resource list for further exploration, and a gratitude journal template for daily practice.

Overall, the structure and key components of the book offer a comprehensive guide for readers to embark on a journey towards a joyful and fulfilled life.

Practical tips for applying the content

1. Set Specific Goals: One of the key components of achieving happiness is setting specific, achievable goals. Utilize the SMART goal-setting framework (Specific, Measurable, Achievable, Relevant, Time-bound) outlined in Chapter 2 to define clear objectives for your personal growth, relationships, mindfulness practices, lifestyle choices, and overall well-being. By breaking down your goals into actionable steps, you can make progress towards a more joyful and fulfilled life.

2. Create a Routine: Consistency is key when it comes to implementing the strategies outlined in each chapter of 'A Happiness Self Help Book.' Establishing a daily or weekly routine that incorporates self-awareness exercises, mindfulness practices, healthy lifestyle choices, and relationship-building activities can help you stay on track and maintain a sense of balance in your life.

3. Practice Gratitude: In Chapter 4, you learned about the benefits of practicing gratitude for enhancing emotional well-being. Incorporate a daily gratitude practice into your routine by keeping a gratitude journal or simply taking a few moments each day to reflect on the things you are thankful for. By focusing on the positive aspects of your life, you can cultivate a more optimistic outlook and increase your overall happiness.

4. Seek Support: Building positive relationships and seeking support from others is crucial for sustaining happiness over time. Reach out to friends, family members, or a therapist for guidance and encouragement as you navigate the challenges and adversities in your life. By fostering a strong support network, you can strengthen your resilience and emotional well-being.

5. Engage in Self-Care: Prioritize self-care practices that nurture your physical, mental, and emotional well-being. Make time for activities that bring you joy and relaxation, such as exercise, meditation, hobbies, or spending time in nature.

Investing in self-care not only boosts your happiness but also enhances your overall quality of life.

6. Reflect and Adjust: Periodically reflect on your progress towards happiness by reviewing your goals, habits, and overall well-being. Use the self-assessment tools provided in the appendices to evaluate your current state and identify areas for improvement. Adjust your strategies and habits as needed to ensure that you are continuously growing and evolving on your path to a joyful and fulfilled life.

7. Celebrate Successes: Acknowledge and celebrate your achievements, no matter how big or small. Recognizing your progress and accomplishments can boost your self-esteem and motivation to continue pursuing happiness. Take time to revel in your successes and milestones, and use them as inspiration to keep moving forward on your journey towards a more joyful and fulfilling life.

By implementing these practical tips for applying the content of 'A Happiness Self Help Book,' you can enhance your well-being, cultivate meaningful relationships, and ultimately achieve a more joyful and fulfilled life. Stay committed to your personal growth and happiness journey, and remember that happiness is a continuous process of self-discovery and growth.

Chapter 1

Understanding Happiness

What is happiness? Various definitions and perspectives

Happiness is a universal concept that has been studied and contemplated by philosophers, psychologists, and everyday individuals throughout history. It is a complex and multifaceted emotion that plays a significant role in shaping our overall well-being and quality of life. In Chapter 1 of 'A Happiness Self Help Book,' we delve into the various definitions and perspectives surrounding happiness to gain a deeper understanding of this elusive yet essential aspect of human experience.

At its core, happiness can be defined as a state of emotional and mental well-being characterized by feelings of contentment, satisfaction, and joy. However, the concept of happiness is subjective and can be understood and experienced differently by each individual. Some may equate happiness with fleeting moments of pleasure and enjoyment, while others view it as a more enduring sense of fulfillment and purpose in life.

From a psychological standpoint, happiness is often associated with positive emotions such as love, gratitude, and peace, as well as a sense of engagement and meaning in one's activities and relationships. Key theories and models, such as Positive Psychology and Hedonic Adaptation, offer valuable insights into the mechanisms that underlie happiness and how individuals can cultivate and sustain it in their lives.

Furthermore, the distinction between happiness and pleasure is an important one to consider. While pleasure is often derived from external stimuli and temporary experiences, happiness is more enduring and rooted in internal factors such as personal values, relationships, and sense of purpose. Understanding this difference can help individuals prioritize long-term well-being over short-term gratification.

Cultural perspectives on happiness also play a significant role in shaping how individuals perceive and pursue happiness. Different cultures may emphasize varying aspects of happiness, such as individual achievement, community harmony, or spiritual fulfillment. Exploring these cultural differences can provide valuable insights into the diverse ways in which people around the world seek to cultivate happiness in their lives.

Moreover, the historical evolution of the concept of happiness reveals how societal attitudes towards well-being have shifted over time. From ancient philosophical teachings on virtue and eudaimonia to modern scientific research on subjective well-being, the understanding of happiness has evolved to encompass a more holistic and multidimensional view of human flourishing.

In conclusion, happiness is a multifaceted and deeply personal experience that encompasses a wide range of emotions, perspectives, and cultural influences. By exploring the various definitions and perspectives on happiness, individuals can gain a more nuanced understanding of what it means to lead a joyful and fulfilled life. Through reflection, self-awareness, and intentional practices, we can cultivate greater happiness and well-being in our daily lives.

The difference between happiness and pleasure

The distinction between happiness and pleasure is a fundamental concept in understanding the complexities of human emotions and well-being. While happiness and pleasure are often used interchangeably in everyday language, they represent distinct emotional states with different underlying mechanisms and long-term effects on our overall quality of life.

Happiness is a broader and more enduring emotional state characterized by a sense of contentment, fulfillment, and overall well-being. It is a deeper and more sustainable feeling that arises from living a meaningful and purposeful life, cultivating positive relationships, and aligning our actions with our values and goals. Happiness is often associated with a sense of inner peace, gratitude, and connection to oneself and others. It is a holistic state that encompasses emotional, psychological, and even spiritual dimensions.

On the other hand, pleasure is a more temporary and superficial experience linked to immediate gratification and sensory indulgence. Pleasure is usually derived from external stimuli such as food, entertainment, or material possessions that provide a fleeting sense of enjoyment or satisfaction. While pleasure can contribute to momentary feelings of happiness, it is often short-lived and may not lead to long-term well-being or fulfillment.

One key difference between happiness and pleasure lies in their underlying motivations. Happiness is typically driven by intrinsic factors such as personal growth, meaningful relationships, and self-actualization, whereas pleasure is often driven by extrinsic factors like material rewards, social approval, or sensory stimulation. This distinction is crucial because relying solely on external sources of pleasure for gratification can lead to a cycle of seeking more and more stimulation without achieving lasting satisfaction or fulfillment.

Moreover, the pursuit of pleasure can sometimes lead to negative consequences such as addiction, impulsivity, and shallow relationships, whereas the pursuit of happiness is associated with greater resilience, self-awareness, and overall life satisfaction. Happiness is a more sustainable and resilient emotional state that can withstand adversity and challenges, whereas pleasure is more vulnerable to fluctuations and external influences.

Understanding the difference between happiness and pleasure can help individuals make more intentional choices in their pursuit of well-being and fulfillment. By prioritizing long-term happiness over short-term pleasure, individuals can cultivate a deeper sense of meaning, purpose, and resilience in their lives. This distinction highlights the importance of investing in activities and relationships that nurture our inner well-being and contribute to a more fulfilling and joyful existence.

In conclusion, while happiness and pleasure are both valuable aspects of human experience, it is essential to recognize their differences and make conscious decisions that prioritize long-lasting well-being and personal growth. By cultivating happiness through meaningful relationships, self-awareness, and purposeful living, individuals can enhance their overall quality of life and experience a deeper sense of fulfillment and contentment.

Psychological and biological aspects of happiness

Psychological and biological aspects of happiness play a crucial role in understanding and achieving a joyful and fulfilled life. Happiness is a complex emotion that involves both psychological and biological components, influenced by various factors such as genetics, brain chemistry, and cognitive processes. In this chapter, we will delve into the intricate interplay between the mind and body in relation to happiness.

Psychologically, happiness is often described as a positive emotional state characterized by feelings of contentment, satisfaction, and well-being. It is influenced by how individuals perceive and interpret their experiences, thoughts, and emotions. Positive psychology, a branch of psychology that focuses on enhancing well-being and happiness, explores the factors that contribute to a fulfilling life, such as positive emotions, engagement, relationships, meaning, and accomplishments.

Biologically, happiness is associated with the release of neurotransmitters and hormones in the brain. For example, dopamine, often referred to as the "feel-good" neurotransmitter, is released in response to rewarding experiences and plays a key role in motivation and pleasure. Serotonin, another neurotransmitter, is involved in regulating mood and emotions, with lower levels linked to depression and anxiety. Endorphins, known as the body's natural painkillers, are released during activities like exercise and laughter, contributing to feelings of euphoria and well-being.

Moreover, research has shown that genetics can influence an individual's predisposition to experiencing happiness. Studies have identified specific genes that may impact an individual's baseline level of happiness, highlighting the genetic component of well-being. However, it is essential to note that while genetics may play a role, happiness is not solely determined by one's genetic makeup. Environmental factors, lifestyle choices, and mindset also significantly contribute to overall happiness levels.

Furthermore, cognitive processes such as perception, attention, memory, and reasoning play a role in shaping one's happiness. Individuals who practice positive thinking, gratitude, and mindfulness tend to experience higher levels of happiness and life satisfaction. Cognitive behavioral therapy (CBT) is a therapeutic approach that focuses on changing negative thought patterns and behaviors to promote emotional well-being and happiness.

In addition to the psychological and biological aspects of happiness, it is essential to consider the influence of social and environmental factors. Social connections, support networks, and a sense of belonging are crucial for fostering happiness and resilience. Creating a positive and supportive social environment can contribute to overall well-being and life satisfaction.

By understanding the psychological and biological aspects of happiness, individuals can cultivate a deeper awareness of their emotional experiences and well-being. Practicing techniques such as mindfulness, gratitude, and positive thinking can help enhance happiness levels and promote a more joyful and fulfilled life. Embracing a holistic approach that considers the interconnectedness of the mind, body, and environment is key to sustaining happiness over time and experiencing lasting well-being.

Key Theories and Models in Understanding Happiness

In the quest to understand happiness, various theories and models have been developed to shed light on the complex and multifaceted nature of this elusive emotion. Two prominent frameworks that have significantly contributed to the study of happiness are Positive Psychology and Hedonic Adaptation.

Positive Psychology:
Positive Psychology is a branch of psychology that focuses on the scientific study of human strengths and virtues, with a specific emphasis on promoting well-being and happiness. Founded by Martin Seligman in the late 1990s, Positive Psychology seeks to shift the traditional focus of psychology from solely treating mental illness to also nurturing positive emotions and character strengths.

One of the core principles of Positive Psychology is the concept of flourishing, which refers to the state of optimal well-being and fulfillment. It emphasizes the importance of cultivating positive emotions, engaging in meaningful activities, nurturing strong relationships, and utilizing personal strengths to lead a fulfilling life.

Positive Psychology also introduces the concept of PERMA model, proposed by Martin Seligman, which outlines five key elements that contribute to well-being:

1. Positive Emotions: Cultivating feelings of joy, gratitude, love, and contentment.

2. Engagement: Immersing oneself in activities that are challenging and rewarding, leading to a state of flow.

3. Relationships: Building and maintaining meaningful connections with others.

4. Meaning: Finding purpose and significance in life through meaningful pursuits.

5. Accomplishments: Setting and achieving goals that align with one's values and passions.

By focusing on these elements, Positive Psychology aims to enhance individuals' overall well-being and happiness by leveraging their inherent strengths and positive qualities.

Hedonic Adaptation:

Hedonic Adaptation, also known as the Hedonic Treadmill, is a psychological phenomenon that refers to the tendency of individuals to return to a baseline level of happiness or well-being, regardless of positive or negative changes in their circumstances. This theory suggests that humans have a natural tendency to adapt to both positive and negative events in their lives, eventually reverting to their previous level of happiness.

According to Hedonic Adaptation, winning the lottery or experiencing a traumatic event may lead to a temporary spike or dip in happiness, but over time, individuals tend to adjust to these changes and return to their baseline level of happiness. This concept highlights the importance of internal factors, such as mindset and attitude, in influencing long-term happiness, as external circumstances have a limited impact on overall well-being.

Understanding Hedonic Adaptation can help individuals manage their expectations and perceptions of happiness, recognizing that lasting fulfillment comes from internal sources rather than external events or possessions. By cultivating gratitude, resilience, and mindfulness, individuals can counteract the effects of adaptation and sustain their happiness levels over time.

In conclusion, Positive Psychology and Hedonic Adaptation offer valuable insights into the complexities of happiness and well-being. By incorporating principles from these theories and models into daily life, individuals can cultivate a deeper understanding of what truly brings them joy and fulfillment, leading to a more meaningful and satisfying existence.

How different cultures view and pursue happiness

Happiness is a universal concept that is interpreted and pursued differently across various cultures around the world. Understanding how different cultures view and seek happiness can provide valuable insights into the diversity of human experiences and shed light on the various paths to a joyful and fulfilled life.

1. Cultural Perspectives on Happiness:

Different cultures have unique perspectives on what constitutes happiness and how it can be achieved. For example, in Western cultures, happiness is often associated with individual achievement, personal success, and material wealth. The pursuit of happiness is seen as a personal journey of self-improvement and fulfillment.

In contrast, Eastern cultures, such as those in Japan and China, may place more emphasis on collective well-being, harmony, and social relationships. Happiness is often viewed as a state of balance and inner peace, achieved through practices like meditation, mindfulness, and connection to nature.

2. Cultural Practices for Happiness:
Cultures around the world have developed various practices and traditions aimed at promoting happiness and well-being. For instance, in Bhutan, a small Himalayan kingdom, the concept of Gross National Happiness (GNH) is prioritized over economic growth. The government measures the well-being of its citizens based on factors like psychological well-being, health, education, and cultural diversity.

In Scandinavian countries like Denmark and Norway, the concept of "hygge" emphasizes coziness, togetherness, and creating a warm atmosphere to promote happiness and contentment. This includes practices like spending time with loved ones, enjoying comfort food, and creating a sense of belonging and community.

3. Cultural Values and Happiness:
Cultural values play a significant role in shaping how individuals perceive and pursue happiness. For example, in collectivist cultures like many Asian societies, relationships and social connections are prioritized over individual success. Happiness is often intertwined with family harmony, community support, and fulfilling social roles.

In individualistic cultures like the United States, personal freedom, autonomy, and self-expression are often seen as key drivers of happiness. Pursuing one's passions, achieving personal goals, and seeking personal fulfillment are commonly valued aspects of happiness in such societies.

4. Cultural Influences on Happiness Strategies:
Cultural beliefs and norms can influence the strategies and methods people use to pursue happiness. For instance, in some cultures, spiritual practices like prayer, meditation, or rituals play a central role in cultivating inner peace and happiness. In other cultures, socializing, community engagement, and acts of kindness towards others are seen as essential for promoting happiness.

Understanding how different cultures view and pursue happiness can broaden our perspectives and offer valuable insights into the diverse ways in which people find meaning and fulfillment in their lives. By exploring these cultural variations, we can learn from each other and adapt effective strategies to enhance our own well-being and lead a more joyful and purposeful life.

Historical shifts in the concept of happiness

Historical shifts in the concept of happiness have been influenced by various philosophical, cultural, and societal factors over the centuries. Understanding these shifts can provide valuable insights into how the perception and pursuit of happiness have evolved over time.

Ancient Philosophical Views: In ancient civilizations such as Greek and Roman societies, happiness was often equated with virtue and living a moral life. Philosophers like Aristotle emphasized the importance of eudaimonia, or flourishing, which involved striving for excellence in all aspects of one's life. Happiness was seen as a byproduct of leading a virtuous and fulfilling life, rather than a fleeting emotional state.

Religious and Spiritual Perspectives: Throughout history, many religious and spiritual traditions have offered their own interpretations of happiness. For example, in Christianity, happiness was often associated with inner peace and contentment derived from a strong faith and connection to God. Similarly, Eastern philosophies like Buddhism and Hinduism emphasized the pursuit of inner peace and enlightenment as the ultimate source of happiness.

Enlightenment and Romanticism: The Enlightenment era in the 17th and 18th centuries brought about a shift in the concept of happiness towards rationalism and individualism. Thinkers like John Locke and Immanuel Kant emphasized the pursuit of personal autonomy and self-determination as key to achieving happiness. The Romantic movement that followed also emphasized the importance of emotional fulfillment and personal expression in the quest for happiness.

Industrialization and Consumerism: The Industrial Revolution and the rise of consumer culture in the 19th and 20th centuries brought about new challenges to the concept of happiness. With the focus shifting towards material wealth and possessions, happiness became increasingly associated with external markers of success and status. This led to a growing sense of disillusionment and discontent as people realized that material wealth alone did not guarantee lasting happiness.

Modern Psychological Perspectives: In the 20th century, the field of psychology began to explore happiness in a more systematic and scientific manner. The emergence of Positive Psychology, pioneered by researchers like Martin Seligman, focused on studying the factors that contribute to well-being and life satisfaction. This shift towards a more evidence-based approach to happiness has helped to debunk some misconceptions and myths surrounding what truly makes people happy.

Globalization and Cultural Influences: In today's interconnected world, the concept of happiness is increasingly influenced by global trends and cultural exchanges. Different cultures have unique beliefs and practices when it comes to happiness, and the rise of social media and technology has made it easier for people to compare their lives to others. This has led to a greater emphasis on individualism and self-expression, but also a growing awareness of the importance of social connections and community for overall well-being.

Overall, the concept of happiness has undergone significant changes throughout history, reflecting the evolving values and priorities of different societies. By understanding these historical shifts, we can gain a deeper appreciation for the complexity of happiness and the diverse paths that can lead to a more joyful and fulfilling life.

Chapter 2

Self-Awareness and Personal Growth

Techniques for understanding your values, strengths, and passions

Techniques for understanding your values, strengths, and passions
Self-awareness is a fundamental aspect of personal growth and happiness. It involves understanding your values, strengths, and passions in order to live a more authentic and fulfilling life. By taking the time to explore and reflect on these aspects of yourself, you can gain clarity on what truly matters to you and what brings you joy and purpose. In this section, we will delve into various techniques for enhancing self-awareness and fostering personal growth.

1. Values Clarification:
Understanding your values is essential for aligning your actions and decisions with what is most important to you. Start by reflecting on what principles and beliefs guide your life. Consider what qualities you admire in others and what behaviors you aspire to embody. Make a list of your core values and rank them in order of importance. This exercise can help you make more intentional choices that are in harmony with your values.

2. Strengths Identification:
Identifying your strengths involves recognizing your unique abilities, talents, and qualities that set you apart. Take a strengths assessment or survey to uncover your top strengths and how you can leverage them in various aspects of your life. Reflect on past experiences where you felt energized and successful, as these instances often highlight your strengths. By focusing on your strengths, you can boost your confidence and performance in pursuit of your goals.

3. Passion Exploration:
Discovering your passions involves exploring activities and interests that ignite your enthusiasm and bring you joy. Make a list of activities that you enjoy and that make you lose track of time. Consider what topics or causes resonate with you on a deeper level. Engage in new experiences and hobbies to uncover hidden passions. By pursuing activities that align with your passions, you can infuse your life with excitement and purpose.

4. Journaling and Reflection:
Journaling is a powerful tool for self-exploration and introspection. Set aside time each day to write about your thoughts, feelings, and experiences. Use prompts such as "What am I grateful for today?" or "What challenges am I facing?" to deepen your self-awareness. Reflect on your values, strengths, and passions in your journal entries to gain insights into your true self. Regular journaling can enhance your emotional intelligence and self-understanding.

5. Feedback and Self-Reflection:
Seek feedback from trusted friends, family members, or mentors to gain external perspectives on your values, strengths, and passions. Ask for specific examples of when they have seen these aspects shine through in your actions. Use this feedback to validate your self-perceptions and identify areas for growth. Engage in regular self-reflection to assess your progress and adjust your goals based on newfound insights.

6. Mindfulness Practices:
Incorporating mindfulness practices, such as meditation and deep breathing exercises, can enhance your self-awareness and emotional regulation. Mindfulness helps you stay present in the moment and observe your thoughts and emotions without judgment. By cultivating a mindful attitude, you can deepen your understanding of your values, strengths, and passions, leading to greater clarity and self-acceptance.

Enhancing your self-awareness through understanding your values, strengths, and passions is a transformative journey towards personal growth and happiness. By investing time and effort into exploring these core aspects of yourself, you can live a more authentic, purposeful, and fulfilling life. Embrace the process of self-discovery and enjoy the profound insights and growth that come with it.

The role of self-awareness in happiness

Self-awareness plays a crucial role in the pursuit of happiness and overall well-being. By understanding oneself on a deeper level, individuals can make more informed decisions, set meaningful goals, and cultivate a sense of authenticity and fulfillment in their lives. In this section, we will explore the significance of self-awareness in happiness and provide practical techniques for enhancing this essential aspect of personal growth.

Self-awareness involves having a clear understanding of one's own personality, emotions, motivations, strengths, and weaknesses. It is the ability to recognize and comprehend your thoughts, feelings, and behaviors in various situations. This introspective awareness allows individuals to make conscious choices that align with their values and aspirations, leading to a more meaningful and fulfilling life.

One of the key benefits of self-awareness in happiness is the ability to identify and pursue goals that are truly meaningful and fulfilling. When individuals have a deep understanding of their values, passions, and strengths, they can set goals that resonate with their authentic selves, leading to a greater sense of purpose and satisfaction. By aligning their actions with their core values, individuals can experience a sense of coherence and harmony in their lives, which contributes to overall well-being.

Self-awareness also plays a critical role in fostering emotional intelligence, which is the ability to recognize, understand, and manage one's own emotions as well as the emotions of others. By being attuned to their own emotions and reactions, individuals can respond to challenges and conflicts in a more constructive and empathetic manner. This emotional awareness allows for healthier relationships, effective communication, and greater resilience in the face of adversity.

Furthermore, self-awareness enables individuals to cultivate authenticity in their interactions and relationships. When individuals are true to themselves and act in alignment with their values and beliefs, they experience a sense of inner peace and contentment. Authenticity fosters genuine connections with others and promotes a deeper sense of belonging and fulfillment in social interactions.

Practical techniques for enhancing self-awareness include mindfulness practices such as meditation, journaling, self-reflection exercises, and seeking feedback from others. These tools can help individuals gain clarity about their thoughts, emotions, and behaviors, leading to a deeper understanding of themselves and their needs. By engaging in regular self-assessment and introspection, individuals can cultivate a strong sense of self-awareness that serves as a foundation for personal growth and happiness.

In conclusion, self-awareness is a fundamental aspect of happiness that empowers individuals to lead more authentic, purposeful, and fulfilling lives. By developing a deep understanding of oneself and cultivating emotional intelligence, individuals can make conscious choices that align with their values, set meaningful goals, and nurture positive relationships. Through self-awareness, individuals can embark on a journey of self-discovery and personal growth that leads to greater happiness, fulfillment, and well-being.

The importance of being true to yourself

The importance of being true to yourself cannot be overstated when it comes to achieving true happiness and fulfillment in life. In Chapter 2 of 'A Happiness Self Help Book', this topic is explored in depth to highlight how self-awareness and personal growth play a crucial role in one's overall well-being.

Being true to yourself means living in alignment with your values, beliefs, passions, and goals. It involves understanding who you are at your core, accepting yourself fully, and making choices that resonate with your authentic self. When you are true to yourself, you experience a sense of inner peace, confidence, and clarity that can positively impact every aspect of your life.

One of the key aspects of being true to yourself is understanding your values. Your values are the guiding principles that shape your decisions and actions. By identifying and honoring your values, you create a sense of purpose and direction in your life. This self-awareness helps you make choices that are in line with what truly matters to you, leading to a greater sense of fulfillment and happiness.

Furthermore, being true to yourself involves acknowledging your strengths and weaknesses. By recognizing your strengths, you can leverage them to achieve your goals and navigate challenges effectively. Embracing your weaknesses with self-compassion allows you to work on areas of improvement without judgment or self-criticism.

Another important aspect of authenticity is staying true to your passions and interests. Engaging in activities that bring you joy and fulfillment is essential for maintaining a sense of happiness and well-being. When you pursue your passions, you experience a deep sense of purpose and vitality that energizes you and enhances your overall quality of life.

In a world where external influences and societal expectations often shape our choices and behaviors, staying true to yourself can be a radical act of self-love and empowerment. It requires courage to stand firm in your beliefs and values, even when faced with criticism or opposition. However, the rewards of living authentically are immeasurable, as you cultivate a strong sense of self-worth and confidence that radiates from within.

Moreover, being true to yourself fosters healthy relationships with others. When you are authentic and genuine in your interactions, you attract like-minded individuals who appreciate and respect you for who you are. This authenticity forms the foundation of meaningful connections and fosters a sense of belonging and acceptance in your social circles.

In conclusion, the importance of being true to yourself cannot be overlooked on the path to happiness and fulfillment. Embracing your authentic self, living in alignment with your values and passions, and honoring your strengths and weaknesses are essential components of self-discovery and personal growth. By staying true to yourself, you cultivate a deep sense of inner harmony and contentment that serves as the cornerstone of a joyful and fulfilling life.

Strategies for Cultivating Authenticity in Daily Life

Authenticity is a key component of living a fulfilling and happy life. When you are true to yourself and live in alignment with your values and beliefs, you experience a sense of inner peace and contentment. Cultivating authenticity requires self-awareness, courage, and a willingness to be vulnerable. Here are some strategies to help you cultivate authenticity in your daily life:

1. Self-Reflection: Take time to reflect on your values, beliefs, and goals. Consider what is truly important to you and what brings you joy and fulfillment. Journaling can be a helpful tool for self-reflection, allowing you to explore your thoughts and emotions in a meaningful way.

2. Practice Mindfulness: Mindfulness involves being present in the moment and paying attention to your thoughts and feelings without judgment. By practicing mindfulness, you can become more aware of your true self and cultivate a deeper sense of authenticity in your interactions with others.

3. Be Honest with Yourself and Others: Authenticity requires honesty and transparency. Be honest about your thoughts, feelings, and intentions with yourself and others. Avoid pretending to be someone you are not or hiding your true self out of fear of judgment.

4. Set Boundaries: Establishing healthy boundaries is essential for cultivating authenticity. Learn to say no to things that do not align with your values or priorities, and communicate your boundaries clearly and assertively with others.

5. Embrace Vulnerability: Authenticity often involves being vulnerable and open with others. Embrace vulnerability as a strength rather than a weakness, and be willing to show your true self, flaws and all.

6. Surround Yourself with Authentic People: Seek out relationships with people who value authenticity and honesty. Surrounding yourself with authentic individuals can inspire and support you in your own journey towards living authentically.

7. Practice Self-Compassion: Be kind and compassionate towards yourself as you strive to live authentically. Accept that authenticity is a process and that it is okay to make mistakes along the way. Treat yourself with the same kindness and understanding that you would offer to a close friend.

8. Engage in Activities that Bring You Joy: Authenticity is closely tied to doing the things that bring you joy and fulfillment. Engage in activities that align with your values and passions, whether it be pursuing a hobby, volunteering for a cause you care about, or spending time with loved ones.

9. Seek Feedback and Support: Ask for feedback from trusted friends or mentors on how you come across to others. Their perspective can provide valuable insights into how authentically you are presenting yourself to the world. Additionally, seek out support from a therapist or counselor if you are struggling to live authentically.

By incorporating these strategies into your daily life, you can cultivate a deeper sense of authenticity and live a more fulfilling and meaningful existence. Remember that authenticity is a journey, not a destination, and that embracing your true self is a powerful step towards achieving lasting happiness and contentment.

How goal-setting contributes to happiness

Goal-setting is a powerful tool that contributes significantly to one's overall happiness and fulfillment in life. In Chapter 2 of 'A Happiness Self Help Book', we delve into the importance of setting meaningful goals and how they can positively impact our well-being.

Setting goals provides us with a sense of direction and purpose. When we have clear objectives to work towards, it gives our lives structure and meaning. This clarity helps us focus our energy and resources on activities that align with our values and aspirations, leading to a greater sense of fulfillment and satisfaction.

Moreover, goal-setting enhances motivation and drive. When we set specific, measurable, achievable, relevant, and time-bound (SMART) goals, we are more likely to be motivated to take action. The process of defining our goals and breaking them down into actionable steps creates a roadmap for success, boosting our confidence and self-efficacy along the way.

By setting goals, we also increase our resilience and perseverance in the face of challenges. When we encounter obstacles or setbacks, having clear goals provides us with the determination to overcome adversity and stay focused on our long-term vision. This resilience not only helps us navigate difficult times but also builds our capacity to adapt and grow in the face of change.

Furthermore, goal-setting fosters a sense of achievement and progress. As we work towards our goals and make incremental steps forward, we experience a sense of accomplishment and satisfaction. Celebrating small wins along the way reinforces our belief in our abilities and fuels our motivation to continue striving towards our larger objectives.

Setting goals can also enhance our self-awareness and personal growth. Through the process of defining our goals, we gain a deeper understanding of our values, strengths, and passions. This self-awareness allows us to set goals that are aligned with our authentic selves, leading to a greater sense of fulfillment and happiness as we pursue objectives that resonate with who we are.

In addition, goal-setting encourages focus and prioritization. In a world filled with distractions and competing demands, having clear goals helps us prioritize what is truly important to us. By focusing our time and energy on activities that support our goals, we can avoid feeling overwhelmed and scattered, leading to a greater sense of control and balance in our lives.

Overall, goal-setting is a fundamental component of achieving happiness and fulfillment. By setting meaningful goals that align with our values, motivations, and aspirations, we create a roadmap for success, enhance our motivation and resilience, foster self-awareness and personal growth, and ultimately experience a greater sense of purpose and satisfaction in our lives.

SMART goals and actionable steps for achieving personal goals

SMART goals are a widely recognized framework for setting and achieving personal goals. The acronym SMART stands for Specific, Measurable, Achievable, Relevant, and Time-bound. By following these guidelines, individuals can increase their likelihood of success and stay motivated throughout the goal-setting process.

Specific: When setting a goal, it is important to be as specific as possible. Instead of a vague goal like "I want to exercise more," a specific goal would be "I will go for a 30-minute walk every morning before work." The more specific the goal, the clearer the path to achieving it becomes.

Measurable: Goals should have a way to track progress and measure success. This could involve setting a target number, time frame, or other quantifiable measurement. For example, if the goal is to drink more water, a measurable target could be "I will drink 8 glasses of water each day."

Achievable: Goals should be realistic and attainable within the individual's current circumstances. Setting goals that are too far out of reach can lead to frustration and demotivation. It's important to consider factors like time, resources, and abilities when setting achievable goals.

Relevant: Goals should align with the individual's values, interests, and long-term objectives. It's essential to ensure that the goal is meaningful and relevant to the individual's overall happiness and well-being. For example, if the goal is to learn a new skill, it should be something that will bring personal satisfaction and growth.

Time-bound: Setting a deadline for achieving a goal creates a sense of urgency and motivation. It helps individuals stay focused and accountable. For example, instead of saying "I want to read more books," a time-bound goal would be "I will read one book per month for the next six months."

Once a SMART goal has been established, it's essential to break it down into actionable steps to make progress towards achieving it. These actionable steps serve as a roadmap and help individuals stay on track. For example, if the goal is to run a 5k race, actionable steps could include:

1. Research and choose a training plan that suits your fitness level.
2. Schedule specific days and times for running sessions each week.
3. Start with shorter distances and gradually increase mileage.
4. Incorporate strength training and stretching exercises to prevent injury.
5. Monitor progress by tracking running times and distances.
6. Seek support from a running group or coach for motivation and accountability.
7. Celebrate milestones along the way, such as completing a certain distance or achieving a new personal best.

By breaking down goals into manageable steps and following the SMART criteria, individuals can increase their chances of success, stay motivated, and ultimately achieve personal growth and fulfillment.

Chapter 3

Building Positive Relationships

The impact of relationships on happiness

Relationships play a crucial role in our overall happiness and well-being. Research consistently shows that strong, positive relationships can have a profound impact on our mental and emotional health. In this chapter, we will explore the various aspects of how relationships influence our happiness and provide practical strategies for building and nurturing positive connections with others.

Impact of Relationships on Happiness:

1. Social Connection: Human beings are inherently social creatures, and our relationships with others are fundamental to our happiness. Strong social connections can provide emotional support, a sense of belonging, and opportunities for shared experiences and joy. Studies have shown that individuals with a strong social support system tend to be happier and more resilient in the face of adversity.

2. Emotional Support: Healthy relationships offer a safe space for sharing our thoughts, feelings, and experiences. Having someone to confide in and lean on during challenging times can significantly impact our emotional well-being. Knowing that we have someone who cares about us and understands us can boost our self-esteem and overall happiness.

3. Sense of Belonging: Feeling connected to others and being part of a community or social group can provide a sense of belonging and purpose. When we feel accepted and valued by others, we are more likely to experience positive emotions and a greater sense of fulfillment in our lives.

4. Quality vs. Quantity: It's not just the number of relationships we have that matters, but the quality of those relationships. Meaningful, supportive, and authentic connections are key to experiencing happiness and well-being. Investing time and effort in nurturing deep and meaningful relationships can lead to greater satisfaction and fulfillment.

Strategies for Building Positive Relationships:

1. Improve Communication: Effective communication is essential for building and maintaining healthy relationships. Practice active listening, empathy, and open, honest communication with your loved ones. Avoid assumptions and misunderstandings by clarifying your thoughts and feelings with others.

2. Cultivate Empathy: Empathy is the ability to understand and share the feelings of another person. By putting yourself in someone else's shoes and showing compassion and understanding, you can strengthen your relationships and create deeper connections with others.

3. Practice Forgiveness: Holding onto grudges and resentment can negatively impact our well-being and relationships. Practice forgiveness as a way to let go of past hurts and move forward with a sense of peace and acceptance. Forgiveness can lead to healing and strengthen your relationships with others.

4. Conflict Resolution: Conflicts are a natural part of any relationship, but how we handle them can make a significant difference in the quality of our connections. Learn effective conflict resolution strategies such as active listening, compromise, and seeking common ground to resolve disputes peacefully and maintain harmonious relationships.

Overall, cultivating positive relationships is essential for our happiness and well-being. By investing time and effort in building strong, supportive connections with others, we can experience greater joy, fulfillment, and resilience in our lives. Prioritize meaningful relationships, communicate openly and authentically, and practice empathy and forgiveness to nurture a positive and nurturing social network that contributes to your overall happiness.

Understanding the quality vs. quantity of relationships

Understanding the quality vs. quantity of relationships is a crucial aspect of fostering happiness and well-being in our lives. In today's fast-paced world, where social media and technology often blur the lines between meaningful connections and surface-level interactions, it is essential to delve deeper into what truly matters when it comes to relationships.

Quality relationships are characterized by genuine emotional connections, mutual respect, trust, and support. These are the relationships that bring joy, fulfillment, and a sense of belonging into our lives. On the other hand, quantity relationships may involve a large number of acquaintances, but lack depth and meaningful interaction.

Research has shown that having a few close and supportive relationships is more beneficial for our mental and emotional well-being than having a large network of superficial connections. Quality relationships provide a sense of security, intimacy, and emotional support that can help us navigate life's challenges and celebrate its joys.

To cultivate quality relationships, it is essential to invest time and effort in nurturing them. This involves active listening, empathy, open communication, and genuine care for the well-being of the other person. Quality relationships are built on a foundation of trust and reciprocity, where both parties feel valued and respected.

On the other hand, focusing solely on quantity relationships may lead to feelings of loneliness, isolation, and disconnection. Superficial interactions and a lack of emotional depth can leave us feeling unfulfilled and craving deeper connections with others.

It is important to evaluate the relationships in our lives and prioritize those that bring us joy, support, and a sense of connection. This may involve setting boundaries with toxic or draining relationships and investing more time and energy in nurturing the relationships that truly matter to us.

In today's digital age, where social media often presents a distorted view of relationships, it is crucial to differentiate between the quantity of connections we have online and the quality of relationships we cultivate in real life. Meaningful interactions, face-to-face conversations, and shared experiences are essential for building strong and lasting relationships.

By focusing on the quality rather than the quantity of relationships in our lives, we can create a supportive and enriching social network that contributes to our overall happiness and well-being. Quality relationships provide a sense of belonging, emotional support, and a deep connection that can enhance our quality of life and bring us lasting joy and fulfillment.

Techniques for Improving Communication with Others

Effective communication is a fundamental aspect of building and maintaining positive relationships, which in turn contributes to our overall happiness and well-being. In this section, we will explore various techniques for improving communication with others, fostering understanding, empathy, and connection.

1. Active Listening:

Active listening is a crucial skill that involves fully engaging with and understanding what the other person is saying. To practice active listening, focus on the speaker without distractions, maintain eye contact, and show interest through nodding or verbal cues. Reflect back what the speaker has said to confirm understanding and provide feedback. Avoid interrupting or formulating your response while the other person is speaking.

2. Empathetic Responses:
Empathy is the ability to understand and share the feelings of another person. When engaging in conversations, strive to respond with empathy by acknowledging the other person's emotions and perspective. Use phrases such as, "I understand how you feel," or "That must have been difficult for you." By demonstrating empathy, you can foster a sense of connection and validation in your interactions.

3. Clear and Open Communication:
Communication is most effective when it is clear, honest, and open. Be transparent in expressing your thoughts and feelings, and avoid vague or ambiguous language that could lead to misunderstandings. Practice assertiveness by expressing your needs and boundaries while respecting the perspectives of others. Encourage open dialogue by creating a safe and non-judgmental environment for sharing.

4. Nonverbal Communication:
Nonverbal cues such as body language, facial expressions, and tone of voice play a significant role in communication. Pay attention to your own nonverbal signals and strive to convey warmth, attentiveness, and respect. Similarly, observe the nonverbal cues of others to better understand their emotions and reactions. Aligning your verbal and nonverbal communication can enhance the clarity and effectiveness of your message.

5. Conflict Resolution Strategies:
Conflicts are a natural part of relationships, but how we navigate and resolve them can impact the quality of our interactions. When faced with conflicts, practice active listening to understand the root causes and perspectives of all parties involved. Use "I" statements to express your feelings and needs without

blaming or accusing others. Collaborate on finding mutually acceptable solutions and be willing to compromise when necessary.

6. Practice Mindful Communication:
Mindfulness can enhance the quality of our communication by promoting presence, awareness, and non-reactivity. Before engaging in conversations, take a moment to center yourself and be fully present with the other person. Listen attentively, without judgment or preconceived notions. Pause before responding to ensure thoughtful and considerate communication. Mindful communication can foster deeper connections and mutual understanding.

By incorporating these techniques into your interactions with others, you can cultivate meaningful and fulfilling relationships that contribute to your overall happiness and well-being. Effective communication is a skill that can be developed and refined through practice and mindfulness, enabling you to connect authentically with others and nurture positive connections in your life.

Active listening and empathetic responses

Active listening and empathetic responses are key components of building positive relationships, fostering understanding, and enhancing communication skills. In Chapter 3 of 'A Happiness Self Help Book', we delve into the importance of active listening and empathetic responses in promoting healthy and fulfilling connections with others.

Active listening is a communication technique that involves fully concentrating on what the speaker is saying, understanding their message, and responding appropriately. It goes beyond simply hearing words to truly comprehending the speaker's emotions, intentions, and underlying meaning. By engaging in active listening, you demonstrate respect, empathy, and genuine interest in the other person's perspective, which can strengthen the bond between individuals and foster mutual trust.

Empathy, on the other hand, is the ability to understand and share the feelings of another person. It involves putting yourself in someone else's shoes, acknowledging their emotions, and responding with compassion and sensitivity. Empathy allows you to connect on a deeper level with others, validate their experiences, and offer support without judgment or criticism.

Practicing active listening and empathetic responses involves several key techniques:

1. Maintaining Eye Contact: By making eye contact with the speaker, you show that you are fully present and focused on their words. This non-verbal cue signals your attentiveness and interest in what they have to say.

2. Reflecting and Paraphrasing: Reflecting back what the speaker has said in your own words demonstrates that you have understood their message. Paraphrasing can clarify any misunderstandings and ensure that both parties are on the same page.

3. Asking Open-Ended Questions: Encourage the speaker to elaborate on their thoughts and feelings by asking open-ended questions that prompt deeper reflection and discussion. This demonstrates your curiosity and willingness to learn more about their perspective.

4. Validating Emotions: Acknowledge the speaker's emotions and validate their feelings without judgment. Show empathy by expressing understanding and compassion for their experiences, even if you may not agree with their point of view.

5. Avoiding Interruptions: Resist the urge to interrupt or interject your own opinions while the speaker is sharing their thoughts. Allow them to express themselves fully before offering your own input or feedback.

6. Expressing Empathy: Demonstrate empathy by acknowledging the speaker's emotions, offering words of support, and showing that you care about their well-being. Empathetic responses create a safe and nurturing environment for open communication and mutual understanding.

By practicing active listening and empathetic responses in your interactions with others, you can cultivate deeper connections, build trust and respect, and create a positive and supportive social network. These skills not only enhance your relationships but also contribute to your own sense of well-being and happiness by fostering meaningful connections with those around you.

The importance of forgiveness for personal happiness

Forgiveness is a powerful tool that plays a crucial role in personal happiness and well-being. In the quest for a joyful and fulfilled life, understanding and practicing forgiveness can have transformative effects on our mental, emotional, and even physical health. This section will delve into the importance of forgiveness for personal happiness, exploring its benefits and providing strategies for incorporating forgiveness into our daily lives.

One of the key reasons forgiveness is essential for personal happiness is that holding onto grudges and resentments can weigh heavily on our hearts and minds. When we harbor negative feelings towards others, it creates a toxic internal environment that can lead to increased stress, anxiety, and even depression. By practicing forgiveness, we release ourselves from the burden of carrying around past hurts and allow ourselves to experience freedom and peace of mind.

Forgiveness also plays a crucial role in maintaining healthy relationships. Conflict and misunderstandings are inevitable in any relationship, but it is how we handle these situations that determines the quality of our connections with others. By practicing forgiveness, we demonstrate empathy, compassion, and understanding towards those who may have wronged us. This not only fosters reconciliation and healing but also strengthens the bonds of trust and intimacy in our relationships.

Furthermore, forgiveness is a key component of self-care and self-compassion. When we forgive ourselves for past mistakes and shortcomings, we cultivate self-acceptance and self-love. This self-forgiveness allows us to let go of guilt and shame, freeing ourselves to move forward with a sense of empowerment and renewal. By practicing self-forgiveness, we nurture a positive self-image and inner peace, which are essential for personal happiness and fulfillment.

In addition to its emotional benefits, forgiveness also has physical health benefits. Research has shown that holding onto anger and resentment can lead to increased blood pressure, heart disease, and other stress-related illnesses. By practicing forgiveness, we reduce the harmful effects of chronic stress on our bodies and promote overall health and well-being.

To incorporate forgiveness into our daily lives, it is essential to cultivate a mindset of empathy and understanding. This involves recognizing that everyone makes mistakes and has their own struggles and challenges. By practicing empathy, we can develop a deeper sense of compassion towards others and ourselves, making it easier to forgive and let go of past grievances.

Practical strategies for practicing forgiveness include journaling about your feelings, expressing your emotions through writing or talking to a trusted friend or therapist, and engaging in forgiveness meditation or visualization exercises. It is also important to set boundaries and communicate your needs in relationships to prevent future conflicts and resentments from arising.

In conclusion, forgiveness is a powerful tool for personal happiness and well-being. By letting go of past hurts, practicing empathy and compassion, and nurturing self-forgiveness, we can experience greater peace, joy, and fulfillment in our lives. Embracing forgiveness as a daily practice can lead to deeper connections with others, improved emotional and physical health, and a renewed sense of self-worth and inner peace.

Strategies for resolving conflicts and maintaining healthy relationships

Building and maintaining positive relationships is a key component of leading a happy and fulfilling life. However, conflicts and challenges are inevitable in any relationship. Learning effective strategies for resolving conflicts and maintaining healthy relationships is essential for promoting harmony and happiness in your personal and professional interactions.

1. Communication is Key: Effective communication lies at the heart of every healthy relationship. It is crucial to express your thoughts, feelings, and needs openly and honestly, while also being receptive to the perspectives of others. Active listening, where you give your full attention to the speaker and seek to understand their point of view, is a fundamental skill in conflict resolution. Practice empathy by putting yourself in the other person's shoes to gain insight into their emotions and motivations.

2. Practice Forgiveness: Holding onto grudges and resentment can poison relationships and hinder your own happiness. Forgiveness is a powerful tool for releasing negative emotions and moving forward. It involves letting go of past grievances and choosing to focus on the present moment. By forgiving others, you free yourself from the burden of anger and resentment, fostering a more positive and harmonious relationship.

3. Conflict Resolution Strategies: When conflicts arise, it is important to address them constructively rather than allowing them to escalate. Avoiding conflicts or resorting to aggression can damage relationships in the long run. Instead, strive to resolve conflicts through open and respectful dialogue. Use "I" statements to express your feelings without blaming the other person. Collaborate on finding mutually acceptable solutions that address the needs and concerns of all parties involved.

4. Set Boundaries: Boundaries are essential for maintaining healthy relationships. Clearly defining your personal boundaries helps establish expectations and prevent misunderstandings. Respect the boundaries of others and communicate your own boundaries assertively. Boundaries create a sense of safety and respect within relationships, fostering trust and mutual understanding.

5. Seek Support: Sometimes, conflicts may be too complex or emotionally charged to resolve on your own. In such cases, seeking the support of a trusted friend, family member, or professional counselor can provide valuable perspective and guidance. A neutral third party can help mediate conflicts and facilitate constructive communication between parties.

6. Cultivate Positivity: Focus on nurturing positive aspects of your relationships and expressing gratitude for the people in your life. Celebrate milestones, show appreciation for small gestures, and express love and kindness regularly. Positivity and appreciation create a strong foundation for healthy relationships and contribute to a sense of connection and fulfillment.

By implementing these strategies for resolving conflicts and maintaining healthy relationships, you can cultivate strong and meaningful connections with others while promoting your own happiness and well-being. Remember that relationships require ongoing effort and communication, but the rewards of fostering positive connections are immeasurable.

Chapter 4

Mindfulness and Emotional Well-being

What is mindfulness and how it contributes to happiness

Mindfulness is a practice that involves being fully present and engaged in the current moment without judgment. It is a state of awareness that allows individuals to observe their thoughts, feelings, and sensations without getting caught up in them. Mindfulness has been shown to have numerous benefits for mental health and overall well-being, including contributing to happiness.

One of the key ways in which mindfulness contributes to happiness is by helping individuals develop a greater sense of self-awareness. By practicing mindfulness, individuals can become more attuned to their thoughts, emotions, and physical sensations, which can lead to a better understanding of their inner workings. This self-awareness can help individuals identify negative thought patterns, unhelpful beliefs, and emotional triggers that may be impacting their happiness. By recognizing these internal factors, individuals can begin to challenge and change them, leading to a more positive and fulfilling state of mind.

Mindfulness also plays a crucial role in helping individuals manage stress and improve emotional well-being. In today's fast-paced and often stressful world, many people struggle to cope with the demands of daily life. Mindfulness practices, such as deep breathing, meditation, and body scans, can help individuals relax their minds and bodies, reduce stress levels, and cultivate a sense of calm and inner peace. By learning to stay present in the moment and let go of worries about the past or future, individuals can experience a greater sense of tranquility and contentment, ultimately contributing to their overall happiness.

Furthermore, mindfulness can enhance the quality of relationships and social interactions, which are important factors in determining one's happiness. By being fully present and attentive during conversations and interactions with others, individuals can improve their communication skills, show empathy and understanding, and strengthen their connections with loved ones. Mindfulness can also help individuals cultivate a sense of gratitude and appreciation for the people in their lives, fostering positive emotions and enhancing feelings of connection and belonging.

In addition, mindfulness practices have been shown to improve cognitive function and enhance emotional regulation. By training the mind to focus on the present moment, individuals can sharpen their attention and concentration, which can lead to increased productivity and efficiency in daily tasks. Moreover, by developing a non-judgmental attitude towards their thoughts and emotions, individuals can learn to respond to challenging situations with greater resilience and emotional balance, reducing the impact of negative emotions on their overall happiness.

Overall, mindfulness is a powerful tool for cultivating a sense of well-being and happiness. By practicing mindfulness regularly, individuals can develop a greater awareness of themselves and their surroundings, manage stress more effectively, improve their relationships, enhance their cognitive abilities, and regulate their emotions. Ultimately, mindfulness can help individuals live more fully in the present moment, appreciate the joys of life, and experience a deep sense of contentment and fulfillment, contributing to their overall happiness and well-being.

Techniques for Incorporating Mindfulness into Daily Life

Mindfulness is a practice that involves being fully present in the moment, with awareness and acceptance of one's thoughts, emotions, and sensations. Incorporating mindfulness into daily life can have significant benefits for overall well-being and happiness. Here are some techniques to help you cultivate mindfulness in your daily routine:

1. Mindful Breathing: One of the simplest and most effective ways to practice mindfulness is through mindful breathing. Take a few minutes each day to focus on your breath, paying attention to the sensation of air entering and leaving your body. This can help you become more grounded and centered in the present moment.

2. Body Scan Meditation: This technique involves systematically focusing on different parts of your body, noticing any sensations or tension you may be holding. By bringing awareness to your physical body, you can release tension and promote relaxation.

3. Mindful Eating: When you eat, do so with full attention to the flavors, textures, and sensations of the food. Avoid distractions like screens or multitasking, and savor each bite mindfully. This can enhance your enjoyment of food and help prevent overeating.

4. Walking Meditation: Instead of rushing through your daily walks, try walking meditation. Focus on the sensation of each step, the movement of your body, and the sights and sounds around you. Walking mindfully can help you feel more connected to your surroundings and reduce stress.

5. Mindful Technology Use: In today's digital age, it's easy to get caught up in constant connectivity and distractions. Practice mindful technology use by taking breaks from screens, setting boundaries with notifications, and being intentional about your online activities.

6. Mindful Communication: Pay attention to your interactions with others by practicing mindful communication. Listen actively, without judgment or interruption, and respond with empathy and compassion. Mindful communication can enhance your relationships and foster deeper connections.

7. Gratitude Practice: Cultivating gratitude is an essential aspect of mindfulness. Take time each day to reflect on things you are grateful for, whether big or small. This practice can shift your focus from negativity to positivity and enhance your overall sense of well-being.

8. Mindful Work: Bring mindfulness into your work environment by taking short breaks for deep breathing, stretching, or meditation. Practice focusing on one task at a time, without distractions, to enhance productivity and reduce stress.

9. Mindful Self-Compassion: Treat yourself with kindness and compassion by practicing self-care and self-compassion. Be gentle with yourself when facing challenges or setbacks, and offer yourself the same understanding and support you would to a friend.

10. Mindful Reflection: End each day with a few moments of mindful reflection. Review your experiences, emotions, and interactions with a non-judgmental attitude. This practice can help you gain insight into your thoughts and behaviors and promote personal growth.

Incorporating mindfulness into your daily life requires practice and consistency. Start with small, manageable steps and gradually incorporate more mindfulness techniques into your routine. By cultivating mindfulness, you can enhance your overall well-being, reduce stress, and cultivate a greater sense of happiness and fulfillment in your life.

Understanding the Impact of Stress on Happiness

Stress is an inevitable part of life, and how we manage it can greatly impact our overall happiness and well-being. In this chapter, we will explore the profound effects of stress on our mental and emotional health, as well as practical tools and strategies for effectively managing and reducing stress to enhance our happiness.

Stress is a natural response to challenging or threatening situations, triggering a cascade of physiological and psychological reactions in the body. While acute stress can be beneficial in motivating us to take action and respond to immediate threats, chronic stress can have detrimental effects on our physical and mental health, including feelings of anxiety, depression, and decreased overall happiness.

One key way that stress impacts happiness is by disrupting our emotional balance. When we are under chronic stress, our bodies are in a constant state of alert, leading to increased levels of cortisol, the stress hormone. This prolonged exposure to stress hormones can impair our ability to experience positive emotions, leading to a reduced capacity for joy and fulfillment in our daily lives.

Furthermore, chronic stress can also affect our cognitive function, making it difficult to focus, concentrate, and make decisions effectively. This can lead to feelings of overwhelm and dissatisfaction, contributing to a sense of unhappiness and dissatisfaction with life.

In addition to its impact on emotions and cognitive function, stress can also manifest physically in the form of tension, headaches, digestive issues, and other health problems. These physical symptoms can further exacerbate feelings of discomfort and unhappiness, creating a vicious cycle of stress and negative emotions.

To effectively manage stress and enhance our happiness, it is essential to develop healthy coping mechanisms and stress management strategies. One powerful tool for reducing stress is mindfulness, which involves being fully present in the moment and observing our thoughts and feelings without judgment. By practicing mindfulness techniques such as deep breathing, meditation, and body scans, we can cultivate a sense of calm and inner peace, reducing the impact of stress on our happiness.

Another effective strategy for managing stress is to engage in regular physical activity. Exercise has been shown to release endorphins, our body's natural feel-good chemicals, which can help alleviate stress and boost our mood. By incorporating regular exercise into our routine, we can improve our overall well-being and resilience to stress, leading to greater happiness and satisfaction in life.

Additionally, building a strong support network of friends, family, or mental health professionals can provide valuable emotional support during times of stress. By reaching out for help and sharing our feelings with others, we can gain perspective, find comfort, and strengthen our connections, enhancing our resilience and capacity for happiness.

In conclusion, understanding the impact of stress on happiness is crucial for cultivating a joyful and fulfilled life. By recognizing the ways in which stress can negatively affect our mental, emotional, and physical well-being, we can proactively implement effective stress management strategies to enhance our resilience, well-being, and overall happiness.

Tools and strategies for stress management

Tools and strategies for stress management are essential components of achieving and maintaining happiness in our lives. Stress is a common and natural response to the challenges and demands we face on a daily basis. However, when stress becomes chronic or overwhelming, it can have detrimental effects on our mental and physical well-being. By incorporating effective stress management techniques into our daily routine, we can better cope with stressors and improve our overall quality of life.

1. Mindfulness Meditation: Mindfulness meditation is a powerful technique for reducing stress and promoting emotional well-being. By focusing on the present moment and observing our thoughts and feelings without judgment, we can cultivate a sense of calm and clarity. Regular practice of mindfulness meditation has been shown to decrease stress levels, improve mood, and enhance overall resilience.

2. Deep Breathing Exercises: Deep breathing exercises can help activate the body's relaxation response, counteracting the physiological effects of stress. By taking slow, deep breaths and focusing on the rhythm of your breathing, you can lower your heart rate, reduce muscle tension, and promote a sense of relaxation and calm.

3. Physical Activity: Regular physical activity is a proven way to reduce stress and improve mental well-being. Exercise releases endorphins, the body's natural mood-boosting chemicals, and helps to reduce levels of stress hormones such as cortisol. Engaging in activities like walking, jogging, yoga, or dancing can provide a healthy outlet for stress and contribute to a more positive outlook.

4. Healthy Lifestyle Choices: Maintaining a healthy lifestyle with proper nutrition, regular exercise, and sufficient sleep is crucial for managing stress. A balanced diet rich in fruits, vegetables, whole grains, and lean proteins can support mood stability and energy levels. Adequate rest and relaxation are also essential for rejuvenating the body and mind, reducing stress, and promoting overall well-being.

5. Time Management and Prioritization: Effective time management and prioritization skills can help reduce feelings of overwhelm and anxiety. By breaking tasks down into manageable steps, setting realistic goals, and establishing priorities, you can create a sense of control and organization in your life. This can help alleviate stress and increase productivity and efficiency.

6. Social Support: Building and maintaining positive relationships with friends, family, and colleagues can provide valuable emotional support during times of stress. Talking to trusted individuals about your feelings and concerns, seeking advice or perspective, and receiving validation and empathy can help alleviate stress and foster a sense of connection and belonging.

7. Relaxation Techniques: Incorporating relaxation techniques such as progressive muscle relaxation, guided imagery, or aromatherapy into your daily routine can help promote relaxation and reduce stress. These techniques can help calm the mind, release tension in the body, and create a sense of peace and tranquility.

8. Seeking Professional Help: In some cases, managing stress may require the support of a mental health professional, such as a therapist or counselor. Therapy can provide a safe and supportive space to explore and address underlying issues contributing to stress, learn coping strategies, and develop resilience skills for managing stress more effectively.

By actively incorporating these tools and strategies for stress management into your daily life, you can enhance your ability to cope with stress, improve your emotional well-being, and cultivate a greater sense of happiness and fulfillment. Remember that managing stress is a continuous process that requires self-awareness, practice, and patience. Prioritize your well-being and make self-care a priority in your daily routine.

The benefits of practicing gratitude

Practicing gratitude is a powerful tool that can significantly enhance your overall sense of well-being and happiness. In Chapter 4 of "A Happiness Self Help Book," we delve into the benefits of incorporating gratitude into your daily routine.

Gratitude is the practice of acknowledging and appreciating the positive aspects of your life, both big and small. Research has shown that cultivating a sense of gratitude can have a profound impact on your mental and emotional well-being. Here are some key benefits of practicing gratitude:

1. Improved Emotional Well-being: Expressing gratitude can help shift your focus from negative thoughts and emotions to those that are positive and uplifting. By regularly reflecting on the things you are grateful for, you can cultivate a more optimistic outlook on life and increase your overall happiness.

2. Reduced Stress and Anxiety: Gratitude has been shown to lower levels of stress and anxiety. When you focus on the things you are thankful for, you are better able to manage challenging situations and cope with adversity in a more constructive way.

3. Enhanced Relationships: Expressing gratitude towards others can strengthen your relationships and foster a sense of connection and appreciation. When you show gratitude towards the people in your life, you not only make them feel valued but also deepen your own sense of fulfillment and belonging.

4. Increased Resilience: Gratitude can help build resilience by shifting your perspective from a focus on what is lacking to what you already have. This can help you bounce back more easily from setbacks and challenges, as you are able to draw upon a sense of gratitude for the positives in your life.

5. Boosted Self-Esteem: Practicing gratitude can boost your self-esteem and self-worth. By acknowledging and appreciating your own strengths and accomplishments, you can cultivate a greater sense of confidence and self-assurance.

6. Better Physical Health: Research has shown that gratitude practices are associated with better physical health outcomes, such as improved sleep quality, reduced inflammation, and a stronger immune system. Grateful individuals tend to engage in healthier behaviors and take better care of themselves.

Incorporating gratitude into your daily routine can be as simple as keeping a gratitude journal, where you write down a few things you are thankful for each day. You can also express gratitude verbally to others, through thank-you notes or acts of kindness. Taking time to reflect on the positive aspects of your life and express appreciation for them can have profound effects on your overall happiness and well-being.

By embracing gratitude as a regular practice, you can cultivate a mindset of abundance and positivity that can transform how you experience the world around you. So, take a moment each day to reflect on the blessings in your life and watch as gratitude helps to elevate your mood, enhance your relationships, and bring greater joy and fulfillment into your life.

Methods for incorporating gratitude into your routine

Incorporating gratitude into your routine is a powerful practice that can significantly enhance your overall sense of well-being and happiness. Gratitude involves acknowledging and appreciating the positive aspects of your life, no matter how big or small. By focusing on gratitude, you shift your perspective from what you lack to what you have, leading to increased feelings of contentment and joy. Here are some effective methods for incorporating gratitude into your daily routine:

1. Gratitude Journaling: One of the most popular and research-backed methods for practicing gratitude is keeping a gratitude journal. Set aside a few minutes each day to write down three to five things you are grateful for. These can be simple things like a beautiful sunset, a kind gesture from a friend, or a delicious meal. Reflecting on and documenting these moments of gratitude can help you cultivate a more positive mindset.

2. Gratitude Meditation: Incorporate gratitude into your mindfulness or meditation practice by focusing on feelings of appreciation and thankfulness. Take a few moments to breathe deeply and reflect on the things in your life that you are grateful for. Visualize these aspects of your life and allow yourself to fully experience the emotions associated with gratitude.

3. Expressing Gratitude to Others: Take the time to express your gratitude to the people in your life who have had a positive impact on you. Whether it's a heartfelt thank-you note, a phone call to express your appreciation, or a small act of kindness in return, showing gratitude to others can deepen your connections and foster a sense of mutual appreciation.

4. Gratitude Walks: Incorporate gratitude into your physical activity routine by going for a gratitude walk. While walking, focus on the beauty of your surroundings, the sensation of movement, and the blessings in your life. Use this time to reflect on the things you are grateful for and let those feelings of appreciation fill you up.

5. Gratitude Rituals: Create daily or weekly gratitude rituals that help you cultivate a mindset of thankfulness. This could be a gratitude prayer before meals, a gratitude reflection before bedtime, or a gratitude sharing session with loved ones. Consistency in practicing gratitude rituals can reinforce the positive impact of gratitude on your well-being.

6. Gratitude Challenges: Challenge yourself to actively seek out moments of gratitude throughout your day. Set a goal to notice and appreciate at least three things each day that bring you joy or make you feel grateful. This can help you train your mind to focus on the positive aspects of your life, even during challenging times.

Incorporating gratitude into your routine is a simple yet transformative practice that can have profound effects on your happiness and overall well-being. By making gratitude a conscious part of your daily life, you can cultivate a more positive outlook, build resilience in the face of adversity, and deepen your sense of fulfillment and contentment. Start small, stay consistent, and watch as the practice of gratitude transforms your life for the better.

Chapter 5

Healthy Lifestyle Choices

How Physical Health Impacts Mental Well-being

Physical health plays a critical role in our overall well-being, encompassing both our physical and mental health. The connection between physical health and mental well-being is profound, with each aspect influencing the other in a reciprocal relationship. In this section, we will explore the ways in which taking care of our bodies can have a significant impact on our mental health and happiness.

1. The Mind-Body Connection:
The mind-body connection is a well-established concept that highlights the interconnectedness of our physical and mental states. Our bodies and minds are intricately linked, and changes in one can affect the other. When we prioritize our physical health through proper nutrition, regular exercise, and sufficient rest, we are also nurturing our mental well-being.

2. Boosting Mood and Energy Levels:
Engaging in regular physical activity has been shown to have a direct impact on our mood and energy levels. Exercise releases endorphins, often referred to as "feel-good" hormones, which can help alleviate symptoms of stress, anxiety, and depression. By incorporating physical activity into our daily routines, we can enhance our overall sense of well-being and vitality.

3. Importance of a Balanced Lifestyle:
Maintaining a balanced lifestyle that includes a nutritious diet, regular exercise, and adequate sleep is crucial for promoting mental wellness. When we fuel our bodies with the nutrients they need and engage in physical activity, we are

supporting our brain health and cognitive function. Additionally, getting enough rest allows our bodies to recharge and rejuvenate, contributing to improved mood and mental clarity.

4. Impact of Diet on Mood:
The food we consume plays a significant role in our mental well-being. Research has shown that certain nutrients, such as omega-3 fatty acids and antioxidants, can have a positive impact on mood and cognitive function. Conversely, diets high in processed foods, sugar, and unhealthy fats have been linked to increased risk of mental health issues such as depression and anxiety. By prioritizing a nutritious and balanced diet, we can support our mental health and emotional resilience.

5. Finding Enjoyable Forms of Exercise:
Exercise does not have to be a chore; finding enjoyable forms of physical activity can make it easier to incorporate into our daily lives. Whether it's dancing, hiking, swimming, or practicing yoga, engaging in activities that bring us joy can enhance the mental health benefits of exercise. By choosing activities that we love, we are more likely to stick with them and experience the positive effects on our mood and well-being.

6. Tips for a Nutritious and Balanced Diet:
A nutritious and balanced diet is essential for supporting both our physical and mental health. Incorporating a variety of whole foods such as fruits, vegetables, whole grains, lean proteins, and healthy fats can provide the nutrients our bodies and brains need to function optimally. In addition, staying hydrated and limiting the consumption of processed foods and sugary beverages can help maintain stable energy levels and mood throughout the day.

In conclusion, prioritizing our physical health is a fundamental aspect of promoting mental well-being and happiness. By nourishing our bodies with nutritious foods, engaging in regular physical activity, and getting enough rest, we can support our overall health and vitality. Making conscious choices to care for our physical well-being can have a profound impact on our mental state, leading to increased happiness, resilience, and overall quality of life.

Creating a balanced lifestyle with diet, exercise, and sleep

Creating a balanced lifestyle with diet, exercise, and sleep is crucial for maintaining overall well-being and happiness. In this section, we will delve into the importance of each component and provide practical tips for incorporating them into your daily routine.

Diet:

A nutritious and balanced diet plays a key role in supporting mental and physical health. Eating a variety of foods rich in essential nutrients such as fruits, vegetables, whole grains, lean proteins, and healthy fats can help fuel your body and mind. Incorporating colorful fruits and vegetables into your meals can provide a range of vitamins, minerals, and antioxidants that support brain function and mood regulation. It is important to limit processed foods, sugary drinks, and excessive amounts of caffeine and alcohol, as these can negatively impact your energy levels and overall well-being.

Exercise:

Regular physical activity is not only beneficial for maintaining a healthy weight and reducing the risk of chronic diseases but also plays a significant role in boosting mood and overall happiness. Engaging in activities such as walking, running, swimming, yoga, or strength training releases endorphins - the body's natural mood elevators, which can help reduce stress, anxiety, and depression. Finding an exercise routine that you enjoy and incorporating it into your daily schedule can have a positive impact on your mental health and well-being.

Sleep:
Quality sleep is essential for cognitive function, emotional regulation, and overall health. Lack of sleep can lead to irritability, poor concentration, and increased stress levels, all of which can impact your happiness and well-being. Aim for 7-9 hours of quality sleep each night by establishing a consistent bedtime routine, creating a relaxing sleep environment, and practicing good sleep hygiene habits such as limiting screen time before bed and avoiding caffeine late in the day. Prioritizing sleep and ensuring you get enough rest can help you feel more energized, focused, and emotionally balanced throughout the day.

Incorporating Balance:
Finding the right balance between diet, exercise, and sleep is key to maintaining a healthy lifestyle. It's important to listen to your body's needs and make adjustments as necessary to ensure you are adequately nourished, physically active, and well-rested. Strive to create a routine that includes nutritious meals, regular physical activity, and consistent sleep patterns to support your overall well-being and happiness.

Practical Tips:
1. Keep a food diary to track your eating habits and identify areas for improvement.
2. Meal prep and plan ahead to ensure you have healthy options available.
3. Find enjoyable forms of exercise that align with your interests and fitness goals.
4. Set a consistent sleep schedule and create a bedtime routine to promote restful sleep.
5. Prioritize self-care and relaxation to reduce stress and improve sleep quality.
6. Seek support from a healthcare professional or nutritionist for personalized advice on diet and exercise.

By prioritizing a balanced lifestyle with attention to diet, exercise, and sleep, you can support your physical and mental well-being, ultimately enhancing your overall happiness and quality of life.

The role of physical activity in boosting happiness

Physical activity plays a crucial role in boosting happiness and overall well-being. The benefits of regular exercise extend far beyond physical health, impacting mental and emotional wellness in profound ways. In this section, we will delve into the various ways in which physical activity can enhance happiness and provide practical tips for incorporating exercise into your daily routine.

One of the primary ways in which physical activity contributes to happiness is through the release of endorphins, often referred to as the "feel-good" hormones. When you engage in exercise, whether it's a brisk walk, a yoga session, or a strength training workout, your body releases endorphins that can uplift your mood and reduce feelings of stress and anxiety. This natural high that comes from physical activity can create a sense of euphoria and overall well-being, leading to a more positive outlook on life.

Furthermore, regular exercise has been shown to improve cognitive function and mental clarity. Physical activity can enhance your focus, concentration, and memory, making it easier to tackle daily tasks and challenges with a clear mind. This cognitive boost can contribute to a sense of accomplishment and satisfaction, further enhancing your overall happiness.

In addition to the immediate mood-boosting effects, engaging in physical activity can also lead to long-term benefits for mental health. Regular exercise has been linked to a reduction in symptoms of depression and anxiety, as well as improved self-esteem and self-confidence. By taking care of your physical health through exercise, you are also nurturing your mental and emotional well-being, creating a strong foundation for a happy and fulfilling life.

Moreover, physical activity can help you build resilience and cope with stress more effectively. When faced with challenges or setbacks, engaging in exercise can provide a healthy outlet for releasing pent-up emotions and tension. The physical exertion of exercise can help you manage stress levels, regulate emotions, and build mental toughness, all of which are essential for maintaining happiness in the face of adversity.

To reap the full benefits of physical activity for boosting happiness, it is important to find forms of exercise that you enjoy and that fit into your lifestyle. Whether it's dancing, hiking, swimming, or practicing martial arts, choosing activities that bring you joy and fulfillment will make it easier to stay motivated and consistent with your exercise routine. Additionally, incorporating variety into your workouts can prevent boredom and keep things interesting, ensuring that you continue to derive pleasure and satisfaction from staying active.

It's also important to set realistic goals and expectations for your physical activity routine. Start small and gradually increase the intensity and duration of your workouts as you build strength and endurance. Remember that consistency is key, so aim to engage in physical activity on a regular basis to experience the full spectrum of benefits for your happiness and well-being.

In conclusion, physical activity plays a vital role in boosting happiness by releasing endorphins, improving cognitive function, enhancing mental health, building resilience, and providing a healthy outlet for stress management. By incorporating regular exercise into your daily routine and choosing activities that bring you joy, you can experience the profound benefits of physical activity on your overall happiness and quality of life.

Finding enjoyable forms of exercise

Finding enjoyable forms of exercise is crucial for maintaining physical health and boosting happiness. Exercise not only improves physical fitness but also has a profound impact on mental well-being. In this section, we will explore the importance of incorporating enjoyable forms of exercise into your routine and provide tips on how to find activities that bring you joy and fulfillment.

Exercise is a fundamental component of a healthy lifestyle, and finding activities that you genuinely enjoy can make it easier to stay motivated and consistent. Engaging in exercise that you find pleasurable can turn physical activity from a chore into a rewarding experience. When you look forward to your workouts, you are more likely to stick to your routine and reap the many benefits that exercise offers.

One of the first steps in finding enjoyable forms of exercise is to explore a variety of activities. Consider trying different types of workouts such as yoga, dance classes, hiking, swimming, cycling, or team sports. Experimenting with different activities can help you discover what resonates with you and what brings you the most satisfaction. Keep an open mind and be willing to step outside of your comfort zone to find new ways to move your body.

It is also essential to consider your personal preferences and interests when choosing an exercise routine. If you enjoy being outdoors, activities like hiking, biking, or running in nature may be particularly appealing. For those who prefer social interaction, group fitness classes or team sports can provide a sense of community and camaraderie. If you value solitude and introspection, activities like yoga or swimming may be more suited to your preferences.

Additionally, incorporating variety into your exercise routine can help prevent boredom and keep your workouts engaging. Mixing up your activities can challenge different muscle groups, prevent plateaus, and stimulate your mind. Consider alternating between cardio, strength training, flexibility exercises, and recreational activities to keep your workouts interesting and enjoyable.

Another important aspect of finding enjoyable forms of exercise is listening to your body and honoring its needs. Pay attention to how different activities make you feel physically and emotionally. Choose exercises that make you feel energized, invigorated, and happy. It's essential to prioritize activities that bring you joy and make you feel good about yourself.

Lastly, remember that exercise should be a source of pleasure and not a source of stress or pressure. Avoid comparing yourself to others or setting unrealistic expectations for your fitness journey. Focus on the intrinsic rewards of movement, such as increased energy, improved mood, and enhanced well-being. Celebrate your progress and achievements, no matter how small, and approach exercise with a mindset of self-care and self-love.

In conclusion, finding enjoyable forms of exercise is an essential aspect of maintaining a healthy and happy lifestyle. By exploring different activities, honoring your preferences, incorporating variety, listening to your body, and focusing on intrinsic rewards, you can create a sustainable and fulfilling exercise routine that contributes to your overall well-being. Remember that exercise is not just about physical fitness but also about cultivating joy, vitality, and happiness in your life.

The Impact of Diet on Mood and Energy Levels

Diet plays a significant role in our overall well-being, affecting not only our physical health but also our mental and emotional states. The foods we consume can have a direct impact on our mood, energy levels, and cognitive function. In this section, we will explore the relationship between diet and happiness, and provide tips for maintaining a nutritious and balanced diet to support your mental well-being.

1. Nutrient-Rich Foods for Better Mood:
Consuming a diet rich in nutrients such as vitamins, minerals, and antioxidants has been shown to positively impact mood and emotional well-being. Incorporating foods like fruits, vegetables, whole grains, lean proteins, and healthy fats can provide the essential nutrients your brain needs to function optimally. For example, foods high in omega-3 fatty acids, such as salmon, walnuts, and flaxseeds, have been linked to improved mood and reduced symptoms of depression.

2. Blood Sugar Regulation for Stable Energy Levels:
Maintaining stable blood sugar levels is crucial for sustaining energy throughout the day and avoiding mood swings. Consuming a balanced diet that includes complex carbohydrates, protein, and fiber can help regulate blood sugar levels and prevent energy crashes. Avoiding sugary foods and refined carbohydrates that cause rapid spikes and crashes in blood sugar can help stabilize your energy levels and promote a more consistent mood.

3. Hydration for Cognitive Function:
Staying hydrated is essential for optimal cognitive function and overall well-being. Dehydration can lead to fatigue, reduced concentration, and mood disturbances. Drinking an adequate amount of water throughout the day can help improve mental clarity, boost energy levels, and support a positive mood. Aim to drink at least 8-10 glasses of water daily to stay hydrated and maintain optimal brain function.

4. Mood-Boosting Nutrients:
Certain nutrients have been found to have mood-boosting properties and can help support emotional well-being. For example, foods rich in magnesium, such as leafy greens, nuts, and seeds, have been linked to reduced symptoms of anxiety and depression. Foods high in vitamin D, such as fatty fish, fortified dairy products, and sunlight exposure, have also been associated with improved mood and mental health.

5. Gut-Brain Connection:
The gut-brain axis is a complex communication network that links the gut microbiota to brain function and mental health. Maintaining a healthy gut microbiome through a diverse and fiber-rich diet can positively impact mood and emotional well-being. Consuming probiotic-rich foods like yogurt, kefir, and sauerkraut can support gut health and may help improve mood and reduce symptoms of depression and anxiety.

In conclusion, the impact of diet on mood and energy levels is significant, highlighting the importance of making healthy food choices to support your overall well-being. By prioritizing nutrient-rich foods, regulating blood sugar levels, staying hydrated, and consuming mood-boosting nutrients, you can enhance your mental health and promote a positive mood. Remember that small changes in your diet can lead to big improvements in your happiness and well-being.

Tips for a Nutritious and Balanced Diet

Maintaining a nutritious and balanced diet is essential for overall health and well-being, including mental and emotional happiness. The foods we consume not only fuel our bodies but also play a significant role in our mood, energy levels, and cognitive function. Here are some tips to help you make informed choices when it comes to your diet:

1. Eat a Variety of Nutrient-Dense Foods:
Include a wide range of nutrient-dense foods in your diet to ensure you are getting all the essential vitamins, minerals, and macronutrients your body needs. Aim to incorporate colorful fruits and vegetables, whole grains, lean proteins, and healthy fats into your meals.

2. Prioritize Whole Foods:
Choose whole, minimally processed foods over highly processed and packaged options. Whole foods are rich in nutrients and fiber, which can help regulate blood sugar levels, support digestion, and promote overall health.

3. Balance Your Macronutrients:
Make sure your meals include a balance of carbohydrates, proteins, and fats. Carbohydrates provide energy, proteins are essential for muscle repair and growth, and fats are important for hormone production and brain function. Opt for complex carbohydrates, lean proteins, and unsaturated fats for optimal health.

4. Stay Hydrated:
Drink plenty of water throughout the day to stay hydrated. Water is essential for proper digestion, nutrient absorption, and overall bodily functions. Limit sugary beverages and opt for water, herbal teas, or infused water for a refreshing and hydrating choice.

5. Monitor Portion Sizes:
Be mindful of portion sizes to prevent overeating and promote a healthy weight. Use smaller plates, chew slowly, and listen to your body's hunger and fullness cues to help regulate your food intake.

6. Include Healthy Snacks:
Choose nutrient-rich snacks such as fruits, nuts, yogurt, or whole-grain crackers to keep your energy levels stable between meals. Avoid reaching for processed snacks high in sugar, salt, and unhealthy fats.

7. Limit Added Sugars and Processed Foods:
Reduce your intake of added sugars, refined grains, and processed foods, which can lead to energy crashes, mood swings, and weight gain. Opt for natural sweeteners like honey or maple syrup and choose whole grains over refined grains.

8. Read Food Labels:
Become familiar with reading food labels to understand the ingredients and nutritional content of the foods you consume. Look for products with minimal ingredients, low added sugars, and high fiber content.

9. Plan Ahead and Prep Meals:
Take the time to plan your meals and snacks in advance to ensure you have healthy options readily available. Meal prepping can help you make nutritious choices throughout the week and avoid impulsive, less healthy food choices.

10. Seek Professional Guidance:
If you have specific dietary needs or health concerns, consider consulting a registered dietitian or nutritionist for personalized advice and guidance. They can help you create a tailored eating plan that meets your nutritional requirements and supports your overall well-being.

By following these tips for a nutritious and balanced diet, you can fuel your body with the nutrients it needs to thrive, support your mental and emotional well-being, and contribute to a happier and healthier lifestyle. Remember that small changes in your diet can have a significant impact on your overall happiness and well-being.

Chapter 6

Finding Purpose and Meaning

Exploring what gives your life meaning and fulfillment

Exploring what gives your life meaning and fulfillment is a crucial aspect of achieving lasting happiness and contentment. In Chapter 6 of 'A Happiness Self Help Book', we delve into the profound journey of self-discovery and purpose-seeking that can lead to a more fulfilling and satisfying life.

To start this exploration, it is important to understand that finding meaning and purpose is a deeply personal and introspective process. What brings meaning and fulfillment to one person may not necessarily resonate with another. This chapter encourages readers to take the time to reflect on their values, passions, and beliefs to uncover what truly matters to them.

Techniques for identifying and pursuing your purpose are discussed in detail. This may involve engaging in activities that align with your values, setting meaningful goals that inspire you, and exploring different avenues that spark joy and fulfillment in your life. By understanding what drives you and what brings you a sense of purpose, you can cultivate a deeper connection to your inner self and create a more meaningful existence.

The chapter also emphasizes the happiness benefits of giving and helping others. Research has shown that acts of kindness and altruism not only benefit the recipients but also contribute to the giver's overall well-being and satisfaction. Engaging in volunteer work, community service, or simply lending a helping hand to those in need can bring a profound sense of fulfillment and purpose to your life.

Moreover, the importance of finding satisfaction in your career or academic pursuits is highlighted. By aligning your work with your passions and values, you can experience a greater sense of purpose and fulfillment in your daily life. Strategies for identifying career paths that resonate with your interests and strengths are discussed, along with practical tips for making the necessary changes to pursue a more fulfilling professional journey.

In addition, opportunities for volunteer work and community involvement are explored as avenues for finding purpose and meaning beyond one's personal endeavors. By actively participating in activities that contribute to the greater good, you can experience a sense of connection, belonging, and purpose that transcends individual achievements.

Lastly, the chapter delves into strategies for aligning your work with your passions and values. By consciously choosing paths that align with your core beliefs and aspirations, you can create a more fulfilling and purpose-driven life. This may involve exploring new career opportunities, pursuing further education or training, or making shifts in your current job to better reflect your values and passions.

In conclusion, exploring what gives your life meaning and fulfillment is a transformative journey that can lead to a deeper sense of happiness and satisfaction. By understanding your values, passions, and purpose, you can create a life that is rich in meaning and purpose, ultimately leading to a more fulfilling and joyful existence.

Techniques for identifying and pursuing your purpose

In the journey towards happiness and fulfillment, one of the key aspects to consider is finding and pursuing your purpose in life. Understanding what gives your life meaning and aligning your actions with that purpose can bring a profound sense of satisfaction and contentment. This chapter will delve into various techniques and strategies to help you identify and pursue your purpose.

Techniques for Identifying Your Purpose:

1. Self-Reflection: Take time to reflect on your values, beliefs, passions, and interests. Consider what activities or pursuits bring you the most joy and fulfillment. Journaling can be a helpful tool in this process, allowing you to explore your thoughts and emotions in a structured way.

2. Seek Feedback: Sometimes, those closest to us can provide valuable insights into our strengths and areas of interest. Ask friends, family members, or mentors for feedback on what they see as your unique qualities and talents.

3. Explore Different Paths: Be open to trying new experiences and stepping out of your comfort zone. Engaging in activities that challenge you and spark your curiosity can help you uncover new aspects of yourself and what truly resonates with you.

4. Connect with Your Inner Child: Think back to what brought you joy and excitement as a child. Often, our childhood interests and dreams hold clues to our deeper passions and purpose in life.

5. Set Meaningful Goals: Identify specific goals that align with your values and passions. When setting goals, consider not only what you want to achieve but also why it is important to you. This can help you clarify your purpose and motivation.

Strategies for Pursuing Your Purpose:

1. Take Action: Once you have identified your purpose or a potential direction, take proactive steps towards pursuing it. Break down your goals into manageable tasks and set a timeline for achieving them.

2. Embrace Challenges: Pursuing your purpose may involve facing obstacles and setbacks along the way. Embrace these challenges as opportunities for growth and learning. Stay resilient and adaptable in the face of adversity.

3. Seek Mentorship: Find mentors or role models who have pursued a similar path or embody qualities you admire. Their guidance and support can be invaluable in helping you navigate your own journey towards purpose and fulfillment.

4. Give Back: Contributing to the well-being of others and making a positive impact in your community can be a powerful way to connect with your purpose. Volunteer work and acts of kindness can enrich your sense of meaning and fulfillment.

5. Align Your Work and Values: If possible, seek opportunities that align with your purpose and values in your career or academic pursuits. Finding meaning in your daily activities can enhance your overall sense of happiness and satisfaction.

By utilizing these techniques and strategies, you can embark on a journey of self-discovery and purposeful living. Remember that finding and pursuing your purpose is a continuous process that may evolve over time. Stay open to new possibilities and experiences, and allow yourself the freedom to explore different paths until you find what truly resonates with your heart and soul.

The happiness benefits of giving and helping others

One of the most fulfilling and rewarding aspects of life is the act of giving and helping others. Research has shown that engaging in acts of kindness and generosity not only benefits the recipients but also has a profound impact on one's own happiness and well-being. In this section, we will explore the various ways in which giving and helping others can contribute to a joyful and fulfilled life.

1. Enhanced Sense of Purpose: Giving to others can provide a sense of purpose and meaning in life. When we contribute to the well-being of others, we feel a sense of fulfillment and satisfaction that goes beyond personal gain. Whether it's volunteering at a local charity, helping a friend in need, or simply offering a listening ear, acts of kindness can give us a greater sense of purpose and direction.

2. Increased Levels of Happiness: Numerous studies have shown that altruistic behaviors are strongly associated with increased levels of happiness and life satisfaction. When we engage in acts of giving and helping, our brains release feel-good chemicals such as dopamine and oxytocin, which are known to boost mood and overall well-being. The act of giving can create a positive feedback loop, leading to greater levels of happiness and fulfillment.

3. Improved Mental Health: Giving and helping others have been linked to improved mental health outcomes, including reduced levels of stress, anxiety, and depression. Engaging in acts of kindness can shift our focus away from our own problems and worries, leading to a greater sense of perspective and gratitude. By helping others, we can foster a sense of connection and belonging that is essential for mental well-being.

4. Strengthened Relationships: Giving and helping others can also strengthen our relationships with friends, family, and the community. When we extend a helping hand to others, we build trust, empathy, and compassion, which are essential components of healthy and fulfilling relationships. By being of service to others, we deepen our connections and create a supportive network of individuals who share our values and goals.

5. Personal Growth and Development: Engaging in acts of giving can also lead to personal growth and self-improvement. By stepping outside of our own needs and desires, we gain a broader perspective on life and develop a greater sense of empathy and compassion. Giving to others can challenge us to step out of our comfort zones, learn new skills, and expand our understanding of the world around us.

In conclusion, the act of giving and helping others is not only a selfless and noble endeavor but also a powerful tool for enhancing our own happiness and well-being. By engaging in acts of kindness and generosity, we can experience a deeper sense of purpose, increased levels of happiness, improved mental health, strengthened relationships, and personal growth. Whether through volunteering, donating, or simply offering a helping hand, the benefits of giving extend far beyond the immediate act itself. As we strive to find meaning and fulfillment in our lives, let us remember the profound impact that giving to others can have on our own happiness and overall well-being.

Opportunities for volunteer work and community involvement

Opportunities for volunteer work and community involvement can play a significant role in enhancing happiness and fulfillment in one's life. Engaging in acts of service and contributing to the well-being of others not only benefits the recipients but also brings a sense of purpose and satisfaction to the volunteer. In this section, we will explore the various ways in which individuals can get involved in their communities and make a positive impact.

Volunteering provides a valuable opportunity to give back to society and make a difference in the lives of others. One of the most common ways to volunteer is through local organizations such as charities, non-profits, and community centers. These organizations often have a range of volunteer opportunities available, from working at events and fundraisers to providing direct services to those in need.

Another avenue for community involvement is through mentorship programs. Becoming a mentor to a young person or someone in need of guidance can be a rewarding experience that not only benefits the mentee but also allows the mentor to share their knowledge and expertise. Mentorship programs can be found in schools, community centers, and youth organizations.

Volunteer work can also extend to environmental initiatives such as participating in clean-up efforts, tree planting projects, or wildlife conservation programs. By taking action to protect the environment and promote sustainability, volunteers contribute to the well-being of the planet and future generations.

In addition to traditional volunteer opportunities, individuals can also get involved in advocacy and social justice causes. This may involve raising awareness about important issues, participating in campaigns and protests, or supporting marginalized communities. By standing up for what they believe in, volunteers can effect positive change and make a lasting impact on society.

Volunteering can also be a form of self-care and personal growth. Engaging in acts of service can help individuals develop empathy, compassion, and a sense of interconnectedness with others. It can provide a sense of fulfillment and purpose that contributes to overall well-being and happiness.

Furthermore, volunteering offers the chance to expand one's social network and build meaningful relationships with like-minded individuals. Working together towards a common goal can foster camaraderie and a sense of community, creating a supportive environment that enhances mental and emotional well-being.

Overall, opportunities for volunteer work and community involvement are plentiful and varied, allowing individuals to find a cause or organization that aligns with their values and interests. Whether it's lending a helping hand to those in need, advocating for social change, or protecting the environment, volunteering offers a fulfilling way to make a positive impact and cultivate happiness in both oneself and others.

Finding satisfaction in your career or academic pursuits

Finding satisfaction in your career or academic pursuits is a crucial aspect of achieving happiness and fulfillment in life. This chapter explores the importance of aligning your work with your passions and values, identifying and pursuing your purpose, and the happiness benefits of giving back to others through your career or academic endeavors.

Exploring What Gives Your Life Meaning and Fulfillment

Identifying what gives your life meaning and fulfillment is the first step towards finding satisfaction in your career or academic pursuits. Take the time to reflect on your values, interests, and passions. Consider what activities or tasks bring you joy and a sense of purpose. By understanding what truly matters to you, you can align your career or academic path with your authentic self.

Techniques for Identifying and Pursuing Your Purpose

Once you have a clear understanding of your values and passions, the next step is to identify your purpose. Your purpose is the overarching goal or mission that guides your decisions and actions. It gives you a sense of direction and fulfillment in your career or academic pursuits. Techniques for identifying your purpose include journaling, seeking mentorship, and engaging in self-reflection exercises.

The Happiness Benefits of Giving and Helping Others

One of the most fulfilling aspects of a career or academic pursuit is the opportunity to give back to others. Whether through volunteering, community involvement, or helping colleagues and peers, contributing to the well-being of others can bring a deep sense of satisfaction and happiness. Research has shown that acts of kindness and generosity can boost your own happiness and well-being.

Opportunities for Volunteer Work and Community Involvement

Engaging in volunteer work and community involvement can provide a sense of purpose and connection to something greater than yourself. Look for opportunities to give back to your community, whether through local organizations, charities, or social initiatives. By contributing your time and skills to those in need, you can experience a profound sense of fulfillment and satisfaction in your career or academic pursuits.

Finding Satisfaction in Your Career or Academic Pursuits

Satisfaction in your career or academic pursuits comes from aligning your work with your passions and values, pursuing your purpose, and giving back to others. Whether you find fulfillment in a creative pursuit, a helping profession, or a challenging academic field, it is essential to prioritize your own happiness and well-being in your professional or academic endeavors.

Strategies for Aligning Your Work with Your Passions and Values

To find satisfaction in your career or academic pursuits, it is important to align your work with your passions and values. Identify what motivates and inspires you, and seek out opportunities that allow you to express your authentic self. Whether through a career change, further education, or personal development, prioritize your own happiness and fulfillment in your professional or academic journey.

In conclusion, finding satisfaction in your career or academic pursuits is a key component of achieving happiness and fulfillment in life. By aligning your work with your passions and values, identifying your purpose, and giving back to others, you can create a meaningful and fulfilling career or academic path that brings you joy and satisfaction. Remember to prioritize your own happiness and well-being in your professional or academic endeavors, and seek out opportunities that allow you to express your authentic self and make a positive impact on the world around you.

Strategies for aligning your work with your passions and values
Finding purpose and meaning in your work is essential for leading a fulfilling and joyful life. When your career aligns with your passions and values, you are more likely to experience greater satisfaction, motivation, and overall happiness. In this chapter, we will explore various strategies to help you align your work with your deepest values and passions.

1. Identify Your Core Values:
Begin by identifying your core values – what truly matters to you in life. This could include values such as integrity, creativity, compassion, or growth. Reflect on your past experiences to pinpoint moments when you felt most fulfilled and aligned with your values. Understanding your values is crucial in guiding your career decisions and ensuring that your work aligns with what is most important to you.

2. Explore Your Passions:
Take the time to explore your passions and interests. What activities or subjects do you find most engaging and enjoyable? Consider how you can incorporate these passions into your work or explore career paths that allow you to pursue

your interests. When you are passionate about your work, it becomes easier to stay motivated and dedicated to your goals.

3. Set Meaningful Goals:
Set clear and meaningful goals that align with your passions and values. These goals should inspire and motivate you, pushing you towards a fulfilling career path. Use the SMART goals framework (Specific, Measurable, Achievable, Relevant, Time-bound) to create actionable steps towards achieving your objectives. Regularly reassess your goals to ensure they remain in alignment with your values and aspirations.

4. Seek Alignment in Your Current Role:
If you are already in a job or career path, assess how well it aligns with your values and passions. Look for opportunities within your current role to incorporate aspects that are meaningful to you. This could involve taking on new projects, seeking mentorship, or advocating for tasks that resonate with your values. By actively seeking alignment in your current role, you can increase your satisfaction and fulfillment at work.

5. Pursue Personal Growth and Development:
Invest in your personal growth and development to enhance your skills and knowledge in areas that align with your passions and values. This could involve enrolling in courses, attending workshops, or seeking mentorship from individuals who share your values. Continuous learning and growth not only benefit your career but also contribute to a sense of fulfillment and purpose.

6. Volunteer and Give Back:
Engaging in volunteer work and giving back to your community can be a powerful way to align your work with your values. Whether through organized volunteer programs or individual acts of kindness, contributing to causes you care about can bring a deeper sense of purpose to your professional life. Look for opportunities to use your skills and expertise to make a positive impact in the world around you.

7. Consider Alternative Career Paths:

If your current job or career does not align with your passions and values, consider exploring alternative career paths that better resonate with who you are. This could involve making a career change, starting your own business, or pursuing a side project that allows you to express your values more authentically. Remember that it is never too late to pursue a career that brings you joy and fulfillment.

In conclusion, aligning your work with your passions and values is a transformative journey that can lead to a more fulfilling and meaningful life. By identifying your core values, exploring your passions, setting meaningful goals, seeking alignment in your current role, pursuing personal growth, volunteering, and considering alternative career paths, you can create a career that resonates with who you are at the core. Embrace this process with openness and dedication, knowing that the pursuit of alignment in your work can bring you closer to a life filled with purpose and happiness.

Chapter 7

Overcoming Challenges and Adversity

Developing Resilience in the Face of Adversity

Resilience is the ability to bounce back from challenges, setbacks, and adversity. It is an essential skill that can help you navigate the ups and downs of life with grace and strength. Developing resilience requires cultivating a mindset that allows you to adapt to difficult circumstances, learn from experiences, and emerge stronger on the other side. In the face of adversity, here are some techniques and strategies you can employ to build and strengthen your resilience:

1. Cultivate a Growth Mindset: Embrace the belief that challenges are opportunities for growth and learning. Instead of viewing setbacks as failures, see them as valuable lessons that can help you become more resilient and resourceful.

2. Practice Self-Compassion: Be kind and understanding towards yourself during tough times. Treat yourself with the same compassion and empathy you would offer to a friend facing adversity. Acknowledge your emotions and allow yourself to feel them without judgment.

3. Seek Support: Reach out to friends, family, or a therapist for emotional support and guidance. Sharing your struggles with others can provide comfort, perspective, and a sense of connection during challenging times.

4. Focus on Solutions: Instead of dwelling on the problem, shift your focus towards finding solutions and taking positive action. Break down overwhelming challenges into smaller, manageable steps and work towards addressing them one at a time.

5. Maintain a Positive Outlook: Cultivate optimism and hopefulness, even in the face of adversity. Remind yourself of past successes and times when you overcame obstacles. Trust in your ability to navigate challenges and believe in a brighter future.

6. Practice Mindfulness: Stay present and grounded in the moment by practicing mindfulness meditation or breathing exercises. Mindfulness can help you manage stress, regulate your emotions, and cultivate resilience in the face of adversity.

7. Learn from Setbacks: View setbacks and failures as opportunities for growth and self-improvement. Reflect on what you can learn from difficult experiences and how you can apply those lessons to future challenges.

8. Adapt to Change: Develop flexibility and adaptability in the face of unexpected events and changes. Embrace uncertainty as a natural part of life and focus on adapting your plans and strategies accordingly.

9. Set Realistic Expectations: Avoid setting unrealistic expectations for yourself and others. Be gentle with yourself and recognize that setbacks and challenges are a normal part of life. Adjust your expectations and goals based on the circumstances you are facing.

10. Practice Gratitude: Cultivate a sense of gratitude for the positive aspects of your life, even during challenging times. Expressing thanks for the small blessings can help shift your perspective towards a more positive and resilient outlook.

By incorporating these strategies into your life, you can develop the resilience needed to face adversity with strength, courage, and grace. Remember that resilience is a skill that can be nurtured and strengthened over time, leading to greater emotional well-being and an increased capacity to overcome life's obstacles.

Techniques for Coping with Challenges and Setbacks

Life is full of ups and downs, and facing challenges and setbacks is a natural part of the human experience. How we respond to these obstacles can greatly impact our overall happiness and well-being. In Chapter 7 of 'A Happiness Self Help Book', we explore various techniques and strategies for coping with challenges and setbacks in a healthy and constructive manner.

1. Develop Resilience:
Resilience is the ability to bounce back from adversity and challenges. Cultivating resilience involves developing a positive mindset, maintaining a sense of perspective, and building a support network. Practice self-care and self-compassion during difficult times, and remind yourself that setbacks are temporary and do not define your worth or capabilities.

2. Practice Acceptance:
Acceptance is key to coping with challenges. Acknowledge the situation for what it is without judgment or resistance. By accepting the reality of the setback, you can begin to focus on finding solutions and moving forward. Avoid dwelling on the past or engaging in negative self-talk, and instead, channel your energy into problem-solving and growth.

3. Seek Support:
During challenging times, it is important to lean on your support system for emotional, practical, and moral support. Reach out to friends, family members, or a therapist for guidance and encouragement. Talking about your feelings and experiences can help you gain perspective and find strength in connection with others.

4. Practice Mindfulness:
Mindfulness is the practice of being present and aware of your thoughts, feelings, and surroundings without judgment. By practicing mindfulness, you

can cultivate a sense of calm and clarity that can help you navigate challenges with greater ease. Engage in mindfulness meditation, deep breathing exercises, or grounding techniques to center yourself during difficult moments.

5. Focus on Solutions:
When faced with a setback, shift your focus from the problem to potential solutions. Break down the challenge into manageable steps and create an action plan to address each aspect. Set realistic goals and timelines for overcoming obstacles, and celebrate small victories along the way. By taking proactive steps towards resolution, you can regain a sense of control and empowerment.

6. Cultivate Optimism:
Optimism is the belief that things will improve and that you have the strength and resources to overcome challenges. Cultivating optimism involves reframing negative thoughts into more positive and hopeful perspectives. Practice gratitude, visualize success, and remind yourself of past achievements to boost your confidence and resilience in the face of adversity.

7. Learn from Setbacks:
Challenges and setbacks offer valuable opportunities for growth and learning. Reflect on the experience and identify lessons that can be applied to future situations. Consider what worked well and what could be improved upon, and use this insight to develop greater resilience and problem-solving skills. Embrace setbacks as stepping stones towards personal development and success.

By incorporating these techniques for coping with challenges and setbacks into your daily life, you can build resilience, cultivate a positive mindset, and navigate obstacles with grace and strength. Remember that setbacks are temporary hurdles on the path to growth and fulfillment, and by facing them with courage and resilience, you can emerge stronger and more resilient than before.

The role of adaptability in maintaining happiness

Adaptability plays a crucial role in maintaining happiness as it allows individuals to navigate life's ups and downs with resilience and grace. In the face of challenges, setbacks, and unexpected changes, those who are adaptable are better equipped to adjust their mindset and behaviors to effectively cope and thrive. This section will explore the significance of adaptability in the pursuit of happiness and provide strategies for developing and enhancing this essential trait.

Adaptability is the ability to adjust to new circumstances, embrace change, and bounce back from adversity. It involves being open-minded, flexible, and resourceful in the face of challenges. When individuals possess a high level of adaptability, they are more likely to maintain a positive outlook, manage stress effectively, and find creative solutions to problems. This adaptive capacity is especially important in today's fast-paced and ever-changing world, where uncertainty and unpredictability are constants.

One key aspect of adaptability is the willingness to learn and grow from experiences. Instead of viewing obstacles as insurmountable roadblocks, adaptable individuals see them as opportunities for personal development and growth. By embracing challenges as learning experiences, they can cultivate a growth mindset that enables them to overcome setbacks and setbacks with resilience and determination.

Furthermore, adaptability allows individuals to navigate transitions and changes in life more smoothly. Whether it's a job loss, a relationship breakup, or a major life event, those who are adaptable can adjust their expectations, priorities, and goals to align with the new reality. This flexibility helps them to maintain a sense of control and agency in their lives, even in the face of uncertainty.

In addition, adaptability fosters emotional well-being by promoting acceptance and self-compassion. Instead of resisting change or dwelling on past failures, adaptable individuals practice self-awareness and self-care, acknowledging their emotions and taking steps to address their needs. This self-compassionate approach allows them to cultivate a positive relationship with themselves, which is essential for overall happiness and well-being.

To enhance adaptability and maintain happiness, individuals can cultivate certain practices and habits. One effective strategy is to practice mindfulness, which involves being present in the moment, non-judgmentally aware of one's thoughts and feelings. Mindfulness helps individuals to stay grounded and centered, even in the face of challenges, enhancing their ability to adapt and respond effectively.

Another helpful practice is to develop problem-solving skills and resilience through cognitive-behavioral techniques. By reframing negative thoughts, setting realistic goals, and seeking support from others, individuals can build their capacity to adapt and thrive in the face of adversity.

Moreover, engaging in activities that promote personal growth and self-discovery, such as journaling, meditation, or pursuing new hobbies, can enhance adaptability by fostering self-awareness and emotional intelligence. These practices help individuals to develop a deeper understanding of themselves and their values, which in turn enables them to navigate life's challenges with greater clarity and purpose.

In conclusion, adaptability is a vital skill for maintaining happiness in the face of life's uncertainties and challenges. By cultivating adaptability through practices such as mindfulness, problem-solving, and personal growth, individuals can enhance their resilience, emotional well-being, and overall satisfaction with life.

Embracing change and uncertainty as opportunities for growth and learning, adaptable individuals can lead more fulfilling and joyful lives.

Strategies for Embracing and Managing Change

Change is an inevitable part of life, and how we navigate through it can greatly impact our overall happiness and well-being. Whether it's a major life transition, a career change, a relationship shift, or simply adapting to new circumstances, learning how to embrace and manage change effectively is crucial for maintaining a sense of balance and fulfillment. Here are some key strategies to help you navigate through change with resilience and positivity:

1. Cultivate a Growth Mindset: Embracing change starts with adopting a growth mindset, which involves viewing challenges as opportunities for learning and growth. Instead of resisting change or viewing it as a threat, try to approach it with curiosity and openness. Understand that change can lead to personal development and new possibilities, and focus on how you can adapt and thrive in the face of uncertainty.

2. Practice Self-Compassion: During times of change, it's important to be kind and compassionate towards yourself. Acknowledge any feelings of fear, anxiety, or discomfort that arise with change, and remind yourself that it's okay to feel vulnerable. Treat yourself with the same level of understanding and support that you would offer to a friend going through a similar situation.

3. Seek Support: Surround yourself with a supportive network of friends, family, or professionals who can provide guidance and encouragement during times of change. Sharing your thoughts and emotions with others can help you gain new perspectives and feel less isolated. Don't hesitate to ask for help when needed, and lean on your support system for reassurance and guidance.

4. Focus on What You Can Control: While change may bring uncertainty and unpredictability, focus on the aspects of the situation that you can control. Identify actionable steps that you can take to navigate through the change effectively, and prioritize those areas where you have agency and influence. By focusing on what you can control, you can regain a sense of empowerment and direction.

5. Practice Mindfulness: Mindfulness can be a powerful tool for managing change, as it helps you stay present and grounded amidst uncertainty. Take time to tune into your thoughts, emotions, and physical sensations without judgment, and cultivate a sense of acceptance and non-reactivity towards the changes happening around you. Mindfulness can help you stay centered and resilient during times of transition.

6. Set Realistic Expectations: It's important to set realistic expectations for yourself during times of change. Understand that adaptation takes time and effort, and that it's okay to experience setbacks or challenges along the way. Be patient with yourself and acknowledge that change is a gradual process that requires perseverance and resilience.

7. Embrace Flexibility: Flexibility is key when navigating through change, as it allows you to adapt to new circumstances and adjust your approach as needed. Be open to exploring different solutions, trying out new strategies, and being willing to pivot when necessary. Embracing flexibility can help you navigate through change with greater ease and adaptability.

8. Reflect and Learn: Use periods of change as opportunities for reflection and self-discovery. Take time to evaluate your experiences, identify lessons learned, and consider how you can apply these insights to future challenges. Embracing change can be a valuable learning experience that helps you grow and evolve as a person.

By incorporating these strategies into your life, you can develop the resilience and adaptability needed to embrace and manage change effectively. Remember that change is a natural part of the human experience, and by approaching it with a positive mindset and proactive attitude, you can navigate through transitions with grace and confidence.

Understanding and managing negative emotions

Understanding and managing negative emotions is a crucial aspect of achieving and maintaining happiness in life. In Chapter 7 of 'A Happiness Self Help Book', we delve into the importance of developing resilience and coping strategies to navigate through challenges and setbacks effectively. Negative emotions are a natural part of the human experience, but how we respond to them can significantly impact our overall well-being and happiness.

The Nature of Negative Emotions

Negative emotions such as sadness, anger, fear, and anxiety are normal responses to various life situations, including stress, disappointment, loss, or conflict. These emotions can serve as important signals that something in our lives needs attention or change. However, when negative emotions become overwhelming or prolonged, they can disrupt our mental and emotional equilibrium, leading to decreased happiness and overall life satisfaction.

Acknowledgment and Acceptance

The first step in managing negative emotions is to acknowledge and accept them without judgment. It is essential to recognize that it is okay to feel upset, frustrated, or anxious at times. By allowing ourselves to experience these emotions fully, we can begin to understand their underlying causes and triggers.

Self-Reflection and Awareness

Self-reflection plays a crucial role in understanding and managing negative emotions. By cultivating self-awareness, we can identify patterns in our emotional responses and thought processes. This awareness helps us recognize when negative emotions arise and how they impact our behavior and well-being.

Healthy Coping Mechanisms

Developing healthy coping mechanisms is essential for managing negative emotions effectively. Engaging in activities such as exercise, mindfulness practices, journaling, or creative pursuits can help regulate emotions and reduce stress levels. It is also important to reach out to supportive friends, family members, or mental health professionals for guidance and assistance when needed.

Cognitive Restructuring

Cognitive restructuring involves challenging and reframing negative thought patterns that contribute to distressing emotions. By questioning irrational beliefs and shifting negative self-talk to more balanced and realistic perspectives, individuals can reduce the intensity of negative emotions and cultivate a more positive mindset.

Emotional Regulation Techniques

Practicing emotional regulation techniques can help individuals cope with intense emotions in a healthy manner. Techniques such as deep breathing, progressive muscle relaxation, or visualization exercises can promote relaxation and reduce emotional reactivity. Mindfulness practices, such as meditation and yoga, can also enhance emotional awareness and resilience.

Seeking Professional Support

In some cases, persistent or overwhelming negative emotions may require professional intervention. Therapists, counselors, or psychologists can provide guidance, support, and evidence-based strategies for managing difficult emotions and developing healthier coping mechanisms. Seeking professional help is a proactive step towards improving emotional well-being and overall happiness.

Conclusion
Understanding and managing negative emotions is a vital skill for navigating life's challenges and fostering happiness and well-being. By acknowledging and accepting negative emotions, cultivating self-awareness, developing healthy coping mechanisms, and seeking support when needed, individuals can effectively manage their emotional responses and cultivate a more positive and fulfilling life. Embracing the full spectrum of emotions, both positive and negative, is a key aspect of the journey towards lasting happiness and emotional resilience.

Tools for transforming negative feelings into positive growth
Transforming negative feelings into positive growth is a crucial aspect of maintaining happiness and overall well-being. Life is full of challenges and setbacks, and it is normal to experience negative emotions such as sadness, anger, frustration, and anxiety. However, learning how to navigate through these emotions and turn them into opportunities for growth and personal development can lead to a more fulfilling and joyful life. In this section, we will explore various strategies and techniques for transforming negative feelings into positive growth.

1. Acknowledge and Accept Your Emotions: The first step in transforming negative feelings is to acknowledge and accept them. Avoid suppressing or denying your emotions, as this can lead to further distress. By recognizing and accepting your feelings, you can begin to understand the root cause of your emotions and work towards addressing them effectively.

2. Practice Self-Compassion: Be kind and compassionate towards yourself during challenging times. Treat yourself with the same empathy and understanding that you would offer to a friend facing similar difficulties. Self-compassion involves recognizing your own humanity, acknowledging your imperfections, and embracing yourself with kindness.

3. Reframe Negative Thoughts: Challenge negative thought patterns by reframing them in a more positive light. Instead of dwelling on self-criticism or pessimism, try to reframe your thoughts with a focus on solutions, growth, and learning opportunities. For example, instead of saying, "I can't do this," reframe it as "I can learn from this experience and improve in the future."

4. Practice Mindfulness: Mindfulness involves being present in the moment and observing your thoughts and emotions without judgment. By practicing mindfulness, you can create space between yourself and your negative feelings, allowing you to respond to challenges with clarity and calmness. Mindfulness techniques such as deep breathing, meditation, and body scans can help you stay grounded during difficult times.

5. Seek Support: Don't hesitate to reach out to friends, family, or a mental health professional for support during challenging times. Talking about your feelings with a trusted individual can provide emotional validation and perspective. Supportive relationships can offer encouragement, guidance, and a sense of connection, which can aid in transforming negative feelings into positive growth.

6. Find Meaning in Adversity: Look for meaning and purpose in difficult situations. Reflect on how challenges can lead to personal growth, resilience, and wisdom. By reframing adversity as an opportunity for growth and learning, you can cultivate a sense of empowerment and optimism in the face of setbacks.

7. Practice Gratitude: Cultivate a mindset of gratitude by focusing on the positive aspects of your life, even during challenging times. Keep a gratitude journal and regularly write down things you are thankful for. Expressing gratitude can shift your perspective towards positivity and increase feelings of happiness and contentment.

8. Engage in Positive Activities: Engage in activities that bring you joy, fulfillment, and a sense of accomplishment. Whether it's pursuing a hobby, spending time in nature, or helping others, participating in positive activities can uplift your mood and foster a sense of well-being. Focus on activities that align with your values and bring meaning to your life.

By implementing these strategies for transforming negative feelings into positive growth, you can cultivate resilience, emotional well-being, and a greater sense of happiness in the face of life's challenges. Remember that setbacks and negative emotions are a natural part of the human experience, and by embracing them with openness and resilience, you can pave the way for personal growth and lasting happiness.

Chapter 8

Creating a Joyful Environment

How Your Physical Environment Affects Your Mood

The environment in which we live and spend our time plays a significant role in shaping our mood, emotions, and overall well-being. Our physical surroundings can have a profound impact on our mental state, influencing our emotions, productivity, and sense of happiness. In this section, we will explore how various aspects of our physical environment can affect our mood and provide practical tips for creating a positive and uplifting living space.

1. Light and Color:
Natural light has been shown to have a positive effect on mood and energy levels. Exposure to natural light can help regulate our circadian rhythms, improve sleep quality, and boost our overall sense of well-being. In contrast, dim or artificial lighting can contribute to feelings of fatigue, lethargy, and even depression.

Color also plays a crucial role in influencing our emotions. Different colors have been found to evoke specific feelings and moods. For example, warm colors like red and orange can create a sense of energy and excitement, while cool colors like blue and green can promote feelings of calmness and relaxation. When designing your living space, consider incorporating colors that align with the mood you want to create in each room.

2. Clutter and Organization:
A cluttered and disorganized environment can lead to feelings of stress, overwhelm, and anxiety. Clutter has been linked to increased levels of cortisol,

the stress hormone, which can have negative effects on both our physical and mental health. On the other hand, an organized and tidy space can promote a sense of calm, clarity, and focus.

Take time to declutter your living space and create systems for organization that work for you. By simplifying your surroundings and keeping things neat and tidy, you can create a more peaceful and harmonious environment that supports your well-being.

3. Nature and Greenery:
Studies have shown that exposure to nature and green spaces can have a positive impact on mood and mental health. Being in natural environments has been linked to reduced stress, improved mood, and increased feelings of well-being. Incorporating plants, flowers, and other elements of nature into your living space can help create a sense of connection to the outdoors and promote a sense of tranquility.

Consider adding indoor plants to your home, placing them in areas where you spend the most time. Not only do plants improve air quality and add visual interest to a space, but they can also have a calming and rejuvenating effect on your mood.

4. Comfort and Personalization:
Creating a comfortable and personalized living environment is essential for promoting a positive mood and overall happiness. Surround yourself with items that bring you joy, whether it's meaningful artwork, photos of loved ones, or cherished mementos. Personalizing your space can create a sense of warmth and familiarity that helps you feel more at ease and content.

Invest in comfortable furniture, soft textiles, and lighting that enhances the ambiance of each room. Create cozy nooks for relaxation and reflection, and design your space in a way that reflects your unique personality and preferences.

By paying attention to the impact of your physical environment on your mood and well-being, you can take proactive steps to create a space that supports your happiness and enhances your quality of life. By incorporating elements that promote light, color, organization, nature, comfort, and personalization, you can cultivate a positive and uplifting living environment that nourishes your mind, body, and spirit.

Tips for creating a positive and uplifting living space

Creating a positive and uplifting living space is essential for fostering happiness and overall well-being. Your environment plays a significant role in shaping your mood, mindset, and energy levels. Here are some practical tips to help you transform your living space into a sanctuary that promotes positivity and joy:

1. Declutter and Organize: Start by decluttering your living space to create a sense of order and harmony. Clutter can contribute to feelings of stress and overwhelm. Organize your belongings and create designated spaces for each item to promote a sense of calm and clarity.

2. Let in Natural Light: Natural light has a powerful impact on mood and well-being. Open up your curtains and blinds to let in as much natural light as possible. If your space lacks natural light, consider adding full-spectrum light bulbs to mimic daylight and boost your mood.

3. Bring Nature Indoors: Incorporating elements of nature into your living space can have a calming and rejuvenating effect. Consider adding houseplants, flowers, or a small indoor garden to bring a touch of greenery into your home. Nature-inspired decor, such as botanical prints or natural materials like wood and stone, can also contribute to a sense of tranquility.

4. Use Color Psychology: Colors have a profound impact on our emotions and energy levels. Choose colors that resonate with you and evoke feelings of positivity and happiness. Soft blues and greens can promote relaxation, while warm yellows and oranges can create a sense of warmth and coziness. Consider painting an accent wall or adding colorful accessories to infuse your space with vibrancy.

5. Personalize Your Space: Surround yourself with items that hold personal meaning and bring you joy. Display photographs of loved ones, artwork that inspires you, or sentimental objects that evoke positive memories. Creating a space that reflects your personality and interests can help foster a sense of comfort and belonging.

6. Create Cozy Spaces: Designate cozy nooks or relaxation areas where you can unwind and recharge. Incorporate soft textiles such as cushions, throws, and rugs to add warmth and comfort to your space. Consider creating a reading corner, meditation space, or a cozy seating area where you can relax and enjoy moments of tranquility.

7. Eliminate Negative Energy: Clear your space of any negative energy by regularly smudging with sage or burning incense. Open windows to allow fresh air to circulate and cleanse the atmosphere. Consider using essential oils or aromatherapy diffusers to create a soothing ambiance and promote relaxation.

8. Foster Positive Vibes: Surround yourself with positive affirmations, inspirational quotes, or uplifting artwork that reinforces a positive mindset. Create a vision board to visualize your goals and aspirations, and place it in a prominent location where you can see it daily. Cultivate an environment that inspires optimism and motivation.

9. Practice Mindfulness: Incorporate mindfulness practices into your daily routine to stay present and appreciate the beauty of your surroundings. Take time to savor moments of relaxation, gratitude, and joy in your living space. Practice deep breathing, meditation, or yoga to cultivate a sense of peace and mindfulness in your home.

By implementing these tips for creating a positive and uplifting living space, you can transform your home into a sanctuary that nurtures your well-being and enhances your overall happiness. Embrace the power of your environment to cultivate a sense of peace, joy, and positivity in your daily life.

Techniques for maintaining a positive outlook

Maintaining a positive outlook is crucial for fostering happiness and overall well-being in life. In Chapter 8 of 'A Happiness Self Help Book,' we explore various techniques and strategies to help you cultivate and sustain a positive mindset despite life's challenges and obstacles.

1. Practice Gratitude: One of the most powerful ways to maintain a positive outlook is by practicing gratitude. Taking time each day to reflect on the things you are grateful for can shift your focus from what is lacking in your life to what you already have. Keeping a gratitude journal or simply making a mental note of three things you are thankful for each day can significantly boost your mood and perspective.

2. Positive Affirmations: Incorporating positive affirmations into your daily routine can help rewire your brain to think more positively. Repeat affirmations such as "I am worthy," "I am capable," or "I choose happiness" to combat negative self-talk and build self-confidence.

3. Surround Yourself with Positivity: Your environment plays a significant role in shaping your outlook on life. Surround yourself with positive influences, whether it be through uplifting music, inspirational books, or spending time with supportive and optimistic people. Avoid toxic relationships and environments that drain your energy and positivity.

4. Mindfulness and Meditation: Practicing mindfulness and meditation can help you stay present in the moment and cultivate a sense of inner peace and calm. By focusing on your breath or observing your thoughts without judgment, you can train your mind to let go of negative thoughts and worries, leading to a more positive outlook on life.

5. Engage in Activities that Bring Joy: Make time for activities that bring you joy and fulfillment. Whether it's pursuing a hobby, spending time in nature, or engaging in creative endeavors, doing things that you love can lift your spirits and help you maintain a positive attitude.

6. Challenge Negative Thinking: Recognize when negative thoughts arise and challenge them with more realistic and positive perspectives. Reframing negative situations as learning experiences or opportunities for growth can help you maintain a positive outlook even in difficult times.

7. Practice Self-Compassion: Treat yourself with kindness and compassion, especially when facing challenges or setbacks. Acknowledge your imperfections and mistakes without harsh self-judgment, and practice self-care activities that nurture your mind, body, and soul.

8. Set Realistic Goals: Setting attainable goals and breaking them down into actionable steps can give you a sense of purpose and accomplishment. Celebrate small victories along the way and adjust your goals as needed to keep yourself motivated and optimistic about the future.

9. Seek Support: Don't hesitate to reach out to friends, family, or a professional counselor if you're struggling to maintain a positive outlook. Talking about your feelings and seeking support can help you gain perspective and find healthy ways to cope with challenges.

By incorporating these techniques for maintaining a positive outlook into your daily life, you can cultivate resilience, optimism, and inner peace that will empower you to navigate life's ups and downs with grace and gratitude. Remember that happiness is a journey, and by nurturing a positive mindset, you can create a more joyful and fulfilling life for yourself and those around you.

The role of optimism in achieving happiness

Optimism plays a crucial role in achieving happiness as it shapes our outlook on life, influences our resilience in the face of challenges, and enhances our overall well-being. In this section, we will delve into the importance of optimism, its impact on happiness, and practical strategies for cultivating a more positive and hopeful mindset.

Optimism is defined as the tendency to expect favorable outcomes and to believe in the best possible future. It is a mindset characterized by hope, positivity, and confidence in one's ability to overcome obstacles and achieve goals. Research in the field of positive psychology has shown that individuals who exhibit a more optimistic outlook tend to experience higher levels of happiness, better physical health, and greater success in various aspects of their lives.

One of the key ways in which optimism contributes to happiness is by influencing how we interpret and respond to life's challenges. Optimistic individuals are more likely to view setbacks as temporary and specific, rather than permanent and pervasive. This cognitive flexibility allows them to bounce back more quickly from adversity, maintain a sense of hope and agency, and continue striving towards their goals despite obstacles.

Moreover, optimism has been linked to improved emotional well-being and mental health. Optimistic individuals tend to experience lower levels of stress, anxiety, and depression, as they are better equipped to cope with negative emotions and maintain a positive perspective even in difficult circumstances. By focusing on the potential for growth, learning, and positive outcomes, optimists can enhance their overall sense of well-being and life satisfaction.

To cultivate optimism and harness its benefits for happiness, there are several practical strategies that individuals can employ:

1. Practice gratitude: Cultivating a sense of gratitude can help shift your focus towards the positive aspects of your life, fostering a more optimistic outlook. Keeping a gratitude journal, regularly expressing appreciation for the people and things you value, and reflecting on moments of joy and abundance can all contribute to a more optimistic mindset.

2. Challenge negative thoughts: Pay attention to your internal dialogue and actively challenge negative or self-defeating beliefs. Replace pessimistic thoughts with more balanced and positive interpretations, reframing challenges as opportunities for growth and learning.

3. Set realistic goals: Establishing clear and achievable goals can provide a sense of purpose and direction, fueling optimism and motivation. Break down larger goals into smaller, actionable steps, and celebrate your progress along the way to maintain a positive momentum.

4. Surround yourself with positivity: Seek out supportive and encouraging relationships, engage in activities that bring you joy and fulfillment, and create a positive environment that uplifts your mood and outlook. Surrounding yourself with positivity can reinforce your optimistic mindset and enhance your overall happiness.

In conclusion, optimism plays a vital role in achieving happiness by shaping our mindset, influencing our responses to challenges, and enhancing our overall well-being. By cultivating a more optimistic outlook through gratitude, positive thinking, goal-setting, and positive surroundings, individuals can harness the power of optimism to cultivate happiness and resilience in their lives. Embracing optimism as a guiding principle can lead to a more fulfilling and joyful existence, characterized by hope, positivity, and a belief in the limitless possibilities for growth and happiness.

Identifying and Pursuing Activities that Bring Joy and Fulfillment

In Chapter 8 of 'A Happiness Self Help Book', the focus shifts to the importance of identifying and pursuing activities that bring joy and fulfillment into our lives. This chapter delves into how our physical environment can impact our mood and overall well-being, and provides practical tips and techniques for creating a positive and uplifting living space. Additionally, it emphasizes the significance of maintaining a positive outlook, the role of optimism in achieving happiness, and the importance of striking a balance between work and leisure for a happier life.

Activities that Bring Joy and Fulfillment:

1. Pursuing Passion Projects: One way to infuse joy and fulfillment into your life is by engaging in activities that align with your passions and interests. Whether it's painting, writing, gardening, or playing music, pursuing passion projects can provide a sense of purpose and fulfillment that goes beyond daily responsibilities.

2. Connecting with Nature: Spending time outdoors and connecting with nature can have a profound impact on your well-being. Whether it's taking a leisurely walk in the park, going for a hike in the mountains, or simply sitting by the beach and watching the waves, immersing yourself in nature can help reduce stress, boost mood, and increase feelings of happiness.

3. Cultivating Relationships: Building and nurturing meaningful relationships with friends, family, and loved ones can bring immense joy and fulfillment into your life. Spending quality time with those who lift you up, support you, and bring positivity into your life can enhance your overall happiness and well-being.

4. Engaging in Acts of Kindness: Giving back to others through acts of kindness, volunteering, or community involvement can not only benefit those in need but also bring a sense of fulfillment and purpose to your own life. Helping others and making a positive impact in the world can contribute to a deeper sense of happiness and satisfaction.

5. Exploring New Hobbies and Interests: Trying out new hobbies, learning new skills, or exploring different interests can spark creativity, curiosity, and a sense of joy. Whether it's taking up photography, learning a new language, or trying a new sport, stepping out of your comfort zone and embracing new experiences can lead to personal growth and fulfillment.

6. Practicing Gratitude: Cultivating a sense of gratitude for the people, experiences, and blessings in your life can enhance feelings of joy and contentment. Keeping a gratitude journal, expressing appreciation to others, or simply taking a moment each day to reflect on the things you are thankful for can shift your focus towards positivity and happiness.

In conclusion, identifying and pursuing activities that bring joy and fulfillment is essential for cultivating a happy and fulfilling life. By incorporating these activities into your daily routine and making time for things that bring you joy, you can enhance your overall well-being, increase your happiness, and create a more meaningful and satisfying life. Remember to prioritize self-care, engage in activities that resonate with your values and passions, and seek out opportunities for growth and connection to sustain happiness over time.

Balancing work and leisure for a happier life

Balancing work and leisure is a crucial aspect of achieving and maintaining happiness in life. In today's fast-paced world, where work tends to consume a significant portion of our time and energy, finding a harmonious equilibrium between work responsibilities and leisure activities is essential for overall well-being. Here is a detailed exploration of how balancing work and leisure contributes to a happier life:

1. Importance of Balance: Balancing work and leisure is vital because it allows individuals to recharge, rejuvenate, and prevent burnout. Engaging in leisure activities provides a much-needed break from the demands of work, allowing for relaxation, creativity, and personal fulfillment. Without a proper balance, individuals may experience increased stress, fatigue, and decreased overall satisfaction with life.

2. Quality vs. Quantity: It's not just about the amount of time spent working or engaging in leisure activities but also about the quality of that time. Balancing work and leisure involves making intentional choices about how time is allocated and ensuring that both work and leisure time are meaningful and fulfilling. This means focusing on productivity and efficiency during work hours and engaging in activities that bring joy and relaxation during leisure time.

3. Setting Boundaries: Establishing clear boundaries between work and leisure is essential for maintaining balance. This may involve setting specific work hours and committing to unplugging from work-related tasks during leisure time. By creating boundaries, individuals can fully immerse themselves in leisure activities without the distractions of work, leading to a more fulfilling experience.

4. Prioritizing Self-Care: Balancing work and leisure also means prioritizing self-care. This includes taking care of physical, emotional, and mental well-being through activities such as exercise, relaxation, hobbies, and spending time with loved ones. Self-care is essential for replenishing energy levels, reducing stress, and enhancing overall happiness.

5. Work-Life Integration: Instead of viewing work and leisure as separate entities, consider integrating them in a way that promotes harmony and fulfillment. This may involve finding ways to incorporate elements of leisure into work, such as taking short breaks to engage in activities that bring joy or pursuing work that aligns with personal passions and values. By integrating work and leisure, individuals can create a more holistic and fulfilling lifestyle.

6. Mindful Time Management: Effective time management is key to balancing work and leisure successfully. By prioritizing tasks, setting realistic goals, and practicing time management techniques, individuals can create space for both work responsibilities and leisure activities. Mindful time management helps prevent feelings of overwhelm and allows for a more balanced and enjoyable daily routine.

7. Creating Joyful Moments: Balancing work and leisure involves consciously creating moments of joy and pleasure in everyday life. This could be as simple as taking a walk in nature during a work break, enjoying a hobby in the evening, or spending quality time with family and friends on weekends. By infusing joy into daily routines, individuals can experience greater happiness and fulfillment.

8. Flexibility and Adaptability: It's important to recognize that achieving a perfect balance between work and leisure is an ongoing process that may require adjustments and flexibility. Life circumstances, work demands, and personal priorities may change, requiring individuals to adapt their routines and priorities accordingly. Being flexible and open to change allows for a more sustainable and adaptable approach to balancing work and leisure.

In conclusion, balancing work and leisure is a dynamic and intentional process that plays a significant role in promoting happiness and overall well-being. By prioritizing self-care, setting boundaries, integrating work and leisure, and creating joyful moments, individuals can achieve a harmonious balance that enhances their quality of life and fosters a sense of fulfillment and contentment. Striking a balance between work and leisure is a valuable investment in personal happiness and long-term well-being.

Chapter 9

Sustaining Happiness Over Time

The Role of Habits in Maintaining Happiness

Habits play a significant role in maintaining happiness and overall well-being in our lives. Habits are the daily routines, behaviors, and actions that we repeatedly engage in without much conscious thought. They shape our daily experiences, influence our mindset, and ultimately impact our happiness levels. Understanding the power of habits and learning how to cultivate positive ones can lead to long-lasting happiness and fulfillment. In this section, we will explore the importance of habits in maintaining happiness and provide strategies for creating and sustaining positive habits.

1. Habits as the Building Blocks of Happiness: Habits are like the building blocks of our daily lives. When we develop positive habits that align with our values and goals, we are more likely to experience a sense of purpose, fulfillment, and joy. By incorporating habits that promote well-being, such as regular exercise, mindfulness practices, and acts of kindness, we can enhance our overall happiness levels.

2. Consistency and Routine: Habits thrive on consistency and routine. When we establish a daily routine that includes positive habits, we create a sense of stability and predictability in our lives. Consistent habits help us feel grounded and in control, which can contribute to a greater sense of happiness and contentment.

3. Creating Positive Habits: To maintain happiness through habits, it is essential to consciously create and nurture positive habits. Start by identifying areas of your life where you would like to see improvement or where you believe positive habits could make a difference. Whether it's incorporating a daily gratitude practice, setting aside time for self-care, or prioritizing healthy eating and exercise, choose habits that align with your values and goals.

4. Behavioral Cues and Rewards: The key to establishing and maintaining habits lies in understanding the habit loop: cue, routine, and reward. Identify a specific cue or trigger that prompts the behavior you want to change or establish. Then, create a routine or action that follows the cue, and finally, reward yourself for completing the routine. By repeating this cycle consistently, you can reinforce positive habits and make them a natural part of your daily life.

5. Breaking Unhealthy Habits: In addition to creating positive habits, it is also important to address and break any unhealthy habits that may be hindering your happiness. Identify negative habits that are contributing to stress, anxiety, or dissatisfaction, and work on replacing them with healthier alternatives. This may require self-reflection, determination, and support from others, but the benefits of breaking harmful habits and replacing them with positive ones are well worth the effort.

6. Accountability and Support: Maintaining happiness through habits can be challenging, especially when faced with obstacles or setbacks. Seek support from friends, family, or a mentor who can help hold you accountable and provide encouragement along the way. Sharing your goals and progress with others can help you stay motivated and committed to cultivating positive habits for long-term happiness.

In conclusion, habits play a crucial role in maintaining happiness by shaping our daily experiences, mindset, and overall well-being. By consciously creating and nurturing positive habits, staying consistent with routines, and seeking support when needed, we can enhance our happiness levels and lead more fulfilling lives. Remember that happiness is not just a destination but a journey that is influenced by the habits we cultivate and the choices we make each day. Start by incorporating small, positive habits into your daily routine and watch as they gradually transform your life for the better.

Strategies for Creating and Sustaining Positive Habits

Developing positive habits is essential for achieving long-term happiness and fulfillment. Habits are the building blocks of our daily routines and behaviors, shaping our overall well-being and success. In this section, we will explore effective strategies for creating and sustaining positive habits that support your journey towards a joyful and fulfilled life.

1. Start Small and Be Consistent: When building new habits, it is crucial to start small and focus on consistency. Begin by choosing one habit that aligns with your goals and values, whether it's practicing gratitude, exercising regularly, or engaging in mindfulness. Consistency is key to forming lasting habits, so commit to practicing your chosen habit daily, even if it's just for a few minutes.

2. Set Clear Goals and Intentions: Clearly define your goals and intentions for the habit you want to cultivate. Make your goals specific, measurable, achievable, relevant, and time-bound (SMART). For example, if you want to incorporate daily exercise into your routine, set a specific goal such as jogging for 30 minutes every morning before work.

3. Create a Routine and Stick to It: Habits thrive in a consistent routine. Design a daily or weekly schedule that includes dedicated time for practicing your new habit. By integrating your habit into your existing routine, such as meditating before bed or journaling in the morning, you make it easier to maintain over time.

Utilize trigger cues and reminders to prompt yourself to engage in your desired habit. This could be setting alarms on your phone, placing visual reminders in your environment, or pairing your habit with an existing routine. For example, if you want to drink more water throughout the day, set reminders on your phone or place a water bottle on your desk as a visual cue.

5. Practice Self-Compassion and Patience: Habits take time to form, and setbacks are a natural part of the process. Be kind to yourself and practice self-compassion when you encounter challenges or slip-ups. Instead of being overly critical, view setbacks as opportunities to learn and grow. Remember that building positive habits is a journey that requires patience and perseverance.

6. Track Your Progress and Celebrate Successes: Keep track of your progress by journaling or using habit-tracking apps. Celebrate small wins and milestones along the way to reinforce your motivation and commitment. Acknowledging your progress and achievements boosts your confidence and reinforces the habit loop.

7. Stay Accountable and Seek Support: Share your goals and progress with a supportive friend, family member, or accountability partner. Having someone to hold you accountable and provide encouragement can help you stay motivated and committed to your habits. Joining a community or group with similar goals can also provide additional support and motivation.

8. Reflect and Adjust as Needed: Regularly reflect on your habits and their impact on your well-being. Assess what is working well and what may need adjustment. If a habit no longer serves you or aligns with your goals, be open to modifying or replacing it with a more beneficial practice. Adaptation and flexibility are key to sustaining positive habits over the long term.

By implementing these strategies for creating and sustaining positive habits, you can cultivate a lifestyle that promotes happiness, resilience, and personal growth. Remember that habits are powerful tools for shaping your daily experiences and overall well-being, so invest time and effort into developing habits that support your pursuit of a joyful and fulfilling life.

Importance of Periodic Self-Assessment and Reflection

Periodic self-assessment and reflection play a crucial role in maintaining happiness and personal growth. By taking the time to evaluate our thoughts, emotions, actions, and progress, we gain valuable insights into our lives and can make necessary adjustments to enhance our overall well-being. In this section, we will explore the importance of self-assessment and reflection and provide practical tips on how to incorporate these practices into your routine.

Self-awareness is the foundation of personal growth and happiness. Through regular self-assessment, we can gain a deeper understanding of ourselves, our values, strengths, weaknesses, and aspirations. This introspective process allows us to identify areas for improvement, set meaningful goals, and align our actions with our values and passions. By reflecting on our past experiences and behaviors, we can learn valuable lessons that help us make better decisions in the future.

Self-assessment also helps us track our progress towards our goals and objectives. By periodically reviewing our achievements and setbacks, we can celebrate our successes, learn from our failures, and adjust our strategies as needed. This ongoing evaluation ensures that we stay focused and motivated on our journey towards happiness and fulfillment.

Reflection is a powerful tool for personal growth and emotional well-being. It allows us to process our thoughts and feelings, gain perspective on challenging situations, and cultivate a sense of gratitude and contentment. By setting aside time for quiet contemplation and introspection, we can reduce stress, improve our mental clarity, and enhance our overall sense of well-being.

Self-assessment and reflection also help us build resilience in the face of challenges and adversity. By acknowledging our strengths and weaknesses, we can develop coping strategies and adaptive mechanisms to navigate difficult times. Reflecting on past experiences of overcoming obstacles can boost our confidence and motivation to tackle new challenges with a positive mindset.

Furthermore, periodic self-assessment and reflection promote continuous learning and personal development. By examining our beliefs, attitudes, and behaviors, we can identify limiting beliefs, biases, and negative patterns that may be holding us back. Through self-reflection, we can challenge our assumptions, expand our perspectives, and cultivate a growth mindset that fosters creativity, innovation, and adaptability.

In conclusion, periodic self-assessment and reflection are essential practices for maintaining happiness and personal growth. By engaging in regular introspection, evaluation, and contemplation, we can deepen our self-awareness, track our progress towards our goals, build resilience in the face of challenges, and promote continuous learning and development. Incorporating self-assessment and reflection into our daily routine can help us live more intentionally, authentically, and joyfully, leading to a more fulfilling and meaningful life.

Adjusting your goals and strategies for continuous improvement

Adjusting your goals and strategies for continuous improvement is a crucial aspect of maintaining happiness and personal growth. In the journey towards a joyful and fulfilled life, it is important to recognize that change is constant, and what once worked for you may not always be the best approach moving forward. By being adaptable and willing to reassess your goals and strategies, you can ensure that you are constantly evolving and progressing towards a better version of yourself.

One key aspect of adjusting your goals is to regularly evaluate your progress and reassess your priorities. This involves taking the time to reflect on your current goals and determining if they are still aligned with your values, passions, and overall vision for your life. By doing so, you can identify areas where you may need to make adjustments or set new goals that better reflect your current desires and aspirations.

Additionally, it is important to be open to feedback and input from others. Seeking advice from mentors, friends, or professionals can provide you with valuable perspectives that can help you see things from a different angle and make more informed decisions about your goals and strategies. Constructive criticism can also highlight areas for improvement that you may not have noticed on your own, allowing you to make necessary changes to enhance your path to happiness.

Another important aspect of adjusting your goals and strategies is being flexible and willing to adapt to changing circumstances. Life is unpredictable, and unexpected challenges or opportunities may arise that require you to pivot and adjust your plans. By staying flexible and open-minded, you can better navigate these changes and continue moving forward towards your goals, even if the path looks different than you initially envisioned.

Furthermore, it is essential to set realistic and achievable goals that are challenging yet attainable. Setting goals that are too easy can lead to complacency, while setting goals that are too ambitious can result in frustration and disappointment. By finding the right balance and regularly adjusting your goals based on your progress and circumstances, you can maintain a sense of motivation and momentum towards your desired outcomes.

In addition to adjusting your goals, it is also important to revisit your strategies for achieving those goals. What may have worked for you in the past may not necessarily be the most effective approach moving forward. By experimenting with different methods, seeking new resources, and learning from your experiences, you can refine your strategies to ensure that they are aligned with your current needs and aspirations.

Overall, adjusting your goals and strategies for continuous improvement is a dynamic and ongoing process that requires self-awareness, adaptability, and a willingness to learn and grow. By regularly reassessing your goals, seeking feedback, staying flexible, setting realistic targets, and refining your strategies, you can ensure that you are on the right path towards sustained happiness and personal fulfillment. Remember, the journey towards happiness is not a one-time event but a lifelong pursuit that requires dedication, resilience, and a commitment to personal growth and improvement.

Recognizing and celebrating your successes and milestones

Recognizing and celebrating your successes and milestones is a crucial aspect of maintaining happiness and motivation in your life. In this section, we will explore the importance of acknowledging your achievements, the positive impact of celebrating milestones, and strategies for effectively recognizing and honoring your successes.

1. Importance of Recognizing Successes:

Recognizing your successes is essential for boosting your self-esteem and self-confidence. Acknowledging your achievements, no matter how big or small, reinforces a positive self-image and encourages further progress towards your goals. By taking the time to reflect on your accomplishments, you build a sense of pride and satisfaction in your abilities and efforts.

2. Positive Impact of Celebrating Milestones:

Celebrating milestones serves as a powerful motivator to continue working towards your aspirations. When you acknowledge and celebrate your successes, you reinforce the belief that your hard work pays off and that you are capable of achieving your dreams. Celebrating milestones also provides a sense of fulfillment and joy, enhancing your overall well-being and happiness.

3. Strategies for Recognizing and Celebrating Successes:

- **Set Clear Goals:** Define specific, measurable goals that you can track and celebrate as you make progress towards them.

- **Acknowledge Small Wins:** Celebrate even the smallest victories along the way to keep yourself motivated and encouraged.

- **Create a Success Journal:** Keep a journal where you record your achievements, milestones, and moments of success to reflect upon during challenging times.

- **Share Your Successes:** Celebrate your successes with loved ones, friends, or colleagues to amplify the joy and positive energy surrounding your achievements.

- **Reward Yourself:** Treat yourself with a meaningful reward or a special activity when you reach a significant milestone or accomplish a goal.

- **Reflect on Your Progress:** Take time to reflect on how far you have come, the obstacles you have overcome, and the growth you have experienced on your journey.

4. Recognizing and celebrating your successes and milestones is an ongoing practice that can greatly enhance your overall happiness and well-being. By acknowledging your achievements, you cultivate a sense of gratitude, self-worth, and motivation to continue striving for personal growth and fulfillment. Remember to celebrate not only the big accomplishments but also the small victories that contribute to your progress and success. By embracing a

mindset of gratitude and celebration, you create a positive and empowering environment that fuels your pursuit of happiness and a joyful life.

The impact of celebration on overall happiness

Celebration plays a crucial role in fostering overall happiness and well-being. By acknowledging and commemorating our successes and milestones, we not only experience a sense of accomplishment and fulfillment but also reinforce positive emotions and behaviors that contribute to our overall happiness. In this section, we will delve into the impact of celebration on our happiness and explore how incorporating regular celebrations into our lives can enhance our overall well-being.

One of the key ways in which celebration contributes to happiness is by boosting our self-esteem and sense of self-worth. When we take the time to celebrate our achievements, no matter how big or small, we validate our efforts and recognize our capabilities. This positive reinforcement helps to build confidence and resilience, empowering us to tackle future challenges with a positive mindset. By acknowledging our successes through celebration, we cultivate a more optimistic and self-assured outlook on life, which in turn enhances our overall happiness.

Moreover, celebration serves as a powerful tool for creating positive memories and experiences. When we mark important milestones or special moments with celebrations, we create lasting memories that we can look back on with joy and gratitude. These positive memories not only contribute to our emotional well-being but also strengthen our social connections and bonds with others. Celebrating together with friends and loved ones fosters a sense of belonging and shared happiness, enhancing our overall sense of fulfillment and satisfaction in life.

In addition, the act of celebration can act as a source of motivation and inspiration for ongoing personal growth and development. By celebrating our achievements, we are reminded of our progress and successes, fueling our motivation to continue striving towards our goals and aspirations. Celebrations can serve as milestones along our journey of self-improvement, providing encouragement and reinforcement to keep moving forward. This continuous cycle of setting goals, working towards them, and celebrating our accomplishments not only boosts our happiness in the present moment but also fuels our long-term fulfillment and sense of purpose.

Furthermore, celebration has a profound impact on our emotional well-being by promoting a positive mindset and enhancing our overall mood. When we take the time to celebrate and express gratitude for the good things in our lives, we shift our focus towards the positive aspects of our experiences and cultivate a sense of appreciation and contentment. This shift in perspective helps to counteract negative emotions and stress, promoting emotional resilience and well-being. By incorporating regular celebrations into our lives, we create a habit of positivity and gratitude that contributes to our overall happiness and life satisfaction.

In conclusion, celebration plays a vital role in nurturing our happiness and well-being by fostering self-esteem, creating positive memories, motivating personal growth, and enhancing our emotional outlook. By embracing the practice of celebration and making it a regular part of our lives, we can cultivate a more joyful and fulfilling existence. Whether it's recognizing our achievements, marking special occasions, or simply expressing gratitude for the blessings in our lives, celebrating the moments that matter can have a profound impact on our overall happiness and quality of life.

Conclusion

Recap of the main strategies and insights for achieving happiness

As we come to the conclusion of 'A Happiness Self Help Book', it is essential to recap the main strategies and insights that have been discussed throughout the book to help you achieve happiness. Happiness is a journey, and by incorporating these strategies into your daily life, you can cultivate a more joyful and fulfilling existence.

1. Understanding Happiness:

The journey to happiness begins with understanding what happiness truly means to you. It is essential to differentiate between happiness and pleasure and to explore the psychological and biological aspects of happiness. By familiarizing yourself with key theories such as Positive Psychology and Hedonic Adaptation, you can gain valuable insights into how to cultivate lasting happiness.

2. Self-Awareness and Personal Growth:

Self-awareness is a crucial component of happiness. By identifying your values, strengths, and passions, you can align your actions with your authentic self. Setting SMART goals and taking actionable steps towards achieving them will contribute to your personal growth and overall happiness.

3. Building Positive Relationships:

Relationships play a significant role in our happiness. Understanding the quality versus quantity of relationships, improving communication skills, practicing forgiveness, and resolving conflicts are all essential aspects of building and maintaining positive relationships that contribute to our well-being.

4. Mindfulness and Emotional Well-being:

Practicing mindfulness can significantly impact your emotional well-being and happiness. Techniques for incorporating mindfulness into your daily life, managing stress effectively, and expressing gratitude can enhance your overall sense of contentment and joy.

5. Healthy Lifestyle Choices:
Taking care of your physical health is essential for mental well-being. Creating a balanced lifestyle through diet, exercise, and sleep can boost your happiness levels. Finding enjoyable forms of exercise, maintaining a nutritious diet, and prioritizing sleep are all key factors in promoting a healthy mind and body.

6. Finding Purpose and Meaning:
Exploring what gives your life meaning and fulfillment is crucial for long-term happiness. By identifying and pursuing your purpose, giving back to others, and aligning your work with your passions and values, you can create a sense of purpose that contributes to your overall happiness.

7. Overcoming Challenges and Adversity:
Developing resilience in the face of challenges is essential for maintaining happiness. By embracing change, managing negative emotions, and transforming setbacks into opportunities for growth, you can navigate life's adversities with grace and strength.

8. Creating a Joyful Environment:
Your physical environment plays a significant role in your mood and outlook on life. By creating a positive and uplifting living space, maintaining a positive mindset, and balancing work and leisure activities, you can cultivate a joyful environment that supports your happiness.

9. Sustaining Happiness Over Time:
Sustaining happiness requires the cultivation of positive habits, periodic self-assessment, and acknowledgment of your successes. By adjusting your goals, reflecting on your progress, and celebrating your achievements, you can maintain a sense of fulfillment and joy over time.

In conclusion, happiness is a multifaceted journey that involves self-awareness, positive relationships, mindfulness, healthy lifestyle choices, finding purpose, resilience, creating a joyful environment, and sustaining happiness over time. By incorporating these strategies into your daily life and staying committed to your pursuit of happiness, you can experience a more joyful and fulfilling existence. Remember, happiness is not a destination but a way of life that requires continuous effort and self-reflection. Stay motivated, stay positive, and continue your journey towards a happier and more fulfilling life.

Motivational message to inspire continued pursuit of happiness

The motivational message in the conclusion of 'A Happiness Self Help Book' serves as a powerful reminder and inspiration for readers to continue their journey towards a joyful and fulfilled life. It encapsulates the essence of the book's teachings and encourages individuals to embrace happiness as a lifelong pursuit. **Here is a detailed 500-word section on the motivational message to inspire continued pursuit of happiness:**

In the final pages of 'A Happiness Self Help Book,' we are reminded that the pursuit of happiness is not merely a destination to reach, but a continuous journey to embark upon. As you reflect on the valuable insights and practical strategies shared throughout this book, it is essential to internalize the message that happiness is not a fleeting emotion to chase after, but a state of being that can be cultivated through intentional actions and mindset shifts.

The motivational message to inspire your continued pursuit of happiness is rooted in the belief that each day presents an opportunity for growth, self-discovery, and joy. It is a call to action to embrace the challenges and triumphs that come your way with resilience, optimism, and an unwavering commitment to your well-being. As you navigate the complexities of life, remember that happiness is not a one-size-fits-all concept but a deeply personal and evolving experience that requires conscious effort and self-awareness.

Take a moment to celebrate how far you have come on your journey towards happiness. Acknowledge the progress you have made, the obstacles you have overcome, and the moments of joy that have illuminated your path. Your resilience in the face of adversity, your commitment to personal growth, and your willingness to cultivate positive relationships are testaments to your inner strength and determination.

As you look towards the future, envision a life filled with purpose, meaning, and fulfillment. Set bold intentions, pursue your passions with unwavering dedication, and embrace the opportunities for growth and transformation that come your way. Remember that happiness is not found in external circumstances or material possessions but in the depth of your connections, the alignment of your values with your actions, and the authenticity of your self-expression.

In moments of doubt or uncertainty, draw upon the wisdom and guidance offered in this book. Reflect on the lessons learned, the tools acquired, and the personal insights gained from each chapter. Revisit the exercises, worksheets, and resources provided to deepen your self-awareness, strengthen your relationships, and nourish your emotional well-being.

Above all, remember that happiness is a choice you make every day. It is a commitment to cultivating gratitude, practicing mindfulness, and nurturing a positive outlook on life. Embrace the power of resilience in the face of challenges, the transformative potential of self-discovery, and the joy that comes from living authentically and purposefully.

In closing, let this motivational message be a beacon of hope and inspiration as you continue your pursuit of happiness. May it remind you of your inherent worth, your limitless potential, and the boundless opportunities for growth and fulfillment that lie ahead. Embrace each day with gratitude, courage, and an unwavering belief in your ability to create a life of joy, meaning, and purpose.

Keep shining brightly on your path towards happiness, knowing that you are capable of creating a life that reflects your true essence and brings you profound fulfillment. The journey towards happiness is not always easy, but it is undoubtedly worth every step taken towards a life lived with intention, authenticity, and unwavering joy.

This motivational message encapsulates the core principles of the book and serves as a powerful reminder for readers to continue their pursuit of happiness with courage, resilience, and unwavering determination.

Suggestions for Further Reading and Resources:

1. "The Happiness Advantage" by Shawn Achor: This book delves into positive psychology and provides practical strategies for achieving greater happiness and success in all areas of life.

2. "The How of Happiness" by Sonja Lyubomirsky: This book offers evidence-based techniques for increasing happiness through intentional activities and habits.

3. "Mindset: The New Psychology of Success" by Carol S. Dweck: Exploring the power of mindset, this book discusses how having a growth mindset can lead to greater happiness and fulfillment.

4. "The Power of Now" by Eckhart Tolle: This spiritual guide emphasizes the importance of living in the present moment and cultivating mindfulness for a more joyful and peaceful life.

5. "Flow: The Psychology of Optimal Experience" by Mihaly Csikszentmihalyi: This book explores the concept of flow and how engaging in activities that challenge and fulfill us can lead to increased happiness.

6. "The Four Agreements" by Don Miguel Ruiz: Offering practical wisdom for personal growth and happiness, this book presents powerful principles for living a fulfilling life.

7. "The Alchemist" by Paulo Coelho: A timeless tale of self-discovery and pursuing one's dreams, this novel inspires readers to find their own path to happiness and fulfillment.

8. "Daring Greatly" by Brené Brown: This book explores the importance of vulnerability and authenticity in building meaningful relationships and living a wholehearted life.

9. "The Art of Happiness" by Dalai Lama and Howard Cutler: A blend of Eastern spirituality and Western psychology, this book offers insights and practices for cultivating lasting happiness and inner peace.

10. "The Science of Happiness" (online course by UC Berkeley's Greater Good Science Center): This course provides a scientific approach to understanding happiness and offers practical tools for increasing well-being.

In addition to these books and resources, consider exploring websites such as Greater Good Magazine, Positive Psychology Program, and Happify for articles, exercises, and tools to further enhance your journey towards a joyful and fulfilled life. Remember, happiness is a journey, and continuous learning and self-improvement play a vital role in sustaining and deepening your sense of well-being.

Appendices

Self-Assessment Tools

Self-assessment tools are powerful resources that can help individuals gain deeper insight into themselves, their values, strengths, and areas for growth. These tools provide a structured approach to self-discovery and goal-setting, enabling individuals to identify what is important to them and how they can align their actions with their values and aspirations. In the context of 'A Happiness Self Help Book', the self-assessment tools included in the appendices are designed to support readers on their journey towards a more joyful and fulfilled life.

One of the key self-assessment tools provided in the book is a Values Assessment Worksheet. This worksheet prompts individuals to reflect on and identify their core values – the principles and beliefs that guide their decisions and actions. By clarifying one's values, individuals can gain a better understanding of what truly matters to them, which in turn can help them make choices that are in alignment with their authentic selves. The Values Assessment Worksheet may include questions such as: "What qualities do I admire in others?", "What activities energize me and make me feel fulfilled?", and "What kind of impact do I want to make in the world?" Through thoughtful reflection and introspection, individuals can uncover their values and use them as a compass for living a more purposeful and meaningful life.

Another valuable self-assessment tool included in the book is a Strengths Finder Exercise. This exercise is designed to help individuals identify their unique strengths and talents – the qualities that come naturally to them and that they can leverage to achieve their goals and aspirations. By recognizing and nurturing their strengths, individuals can boost their self-confidence, enhance their performance, and experience a greater sense of fulfillment in their endeavors. The Strengths Finder Exercise may involve activities such as reflecting on past successes, seeking feedback from others, and engaging in self-awareness exercises to pinpoint areas of excellence and potential for growth.

In addition to values assessment and strengths identification, the self-assessment tools in 'A Happiness Self Help Book' may also include exercises for goal-setting and action planning. These tools enable individuals to translate their self-discoveries into concrete steps for personal growth and development. By setting specific, measurable, achievable, relevant, and time-bound (SMART) goals, individuals can create a roadmap for success and track their progress towards a more joyful and fulfilling life. Goal-setting exercises may involve defining short-term and long-term objectives, breaking them down into actionable steps, and establishing accountability mechanisms to stay on track.

Overall, the self-assessment tools provided in the book offer readers a structured framework for self-discovery and goal-setting, empowering them to cultivate authenticity, leverage their strengths, and align their actions with their values and aspirations. By engaging with these tools thoughtfully and consistently, individuals can gain clarity about who they are, what they want, and how they can create a life filled with happiness and fulfillment.

Resource List

The Resource List section of 'A Happiness Self Help Book' provides readers with a curated selection of recommended books, websites, and apps to further explore the concepts and strategies discussed in the book. These resources offer additional insights, tools, and guidance to support individuals on their journey towards a happier and more fulfilled life.

Recommended Books:

1. **"The Happiness Project" by Gretchen Rubin** - This book offers a practical and engaging approach to exploring happiness and making positive changes in your life.

2. **"Flow: The Psychology of Optimal Experience" by Mihaly Csikszentmihalyi** - Csikszentmihalyi explores the concept of 'flow' and how engaging in activities that challenge and excite us can lead to greater happiness.

3. **"The Power of Now: A Guide to Spiritual Enlightenment" by Eckhart Tolle** - Tolle's book emphasizes the importance of mindfulness and living in the present moment for finding peace and happiness.

4. **"Daring Greatly: How the Courage to Be Vulnerable Transforms the Way We Live, Love, Parent, and Lead" by Brené Brown** - Brown's work on vulnerability and authenticity can help readers build stronger relationships and live more fulfilling lives.

Recommended Websites:

1. **Greater Good Science Center (greatergood.berkeley.edu)** - This website offers research-based articles and resources on happiness, compassion, and well-being.

2. **Positive Psychology Program (positivepsychology.com)** - A comprehensive resource for learning about positive psychology theories and practical exercises to enhance happiness.

3. **Tiny Buddha (tinybuddha.com)** - A community website that shares personal stories, insights, and practical tips for living a more mindful and meaningful life.

4. Happify (happify.com) - An app-based platform that offers science-backed activities and games to boost happiness and reduce stress.

Recommended Apps:

1. Headspace - A meditation and mindfulness app that provides guided sessions to help users cultivate mindfulness and reduce stress.

2. Calm - An app offering guided meditations, sleep stories, and relaxation techniques to promote emotional well-being and better sleep.

3. Gratitude Journal - An app that prompts users to practice daily gratitude by recording moments of appreciation and positivity in their lives.

4. Insight Timer - A meditation app with a diverse collection of guided meditations, music tracks, and talks to support mental health and well-being.

By exploring these recommended resources, readers can deepen their understanding of happiness, personal growth, relationships, mindfulness, healthy lifestyle choices, purpose, resilience, and creating a joyful environment. These books, websites, and apps offer valuable tools and insights to support individuals in their pursuit of lasting happiness and fulfillment.

Gratitude Journal Template

A gratitude journal is a powerful tool that can help cultivate a positive mindset, enhance emotional well-being, and promote overall happiness. Keeping a gratitude journal involves regularly recording things you are grateful for, whether big or small, and reflecting on the positive aspects of your life. The following is a sample template for a daily gratitude practice that you can use to start incorporating gratitude into your routine:

1. Date: Begin each entry by writing down the date to track your progress and see how your gratitude practice evolves over time.

2. Three Things I Am Grateful For Today: List three things that you are grateful for on that particular day. These can be anything from simple pleasures like a warm cup of tea in the morning to significant events like a supportive friend or a fulfilling accomplishment.

3. Why I Am Grateful: For each item on your gratitude list, take a moment to reflect on why you are grateful for it. This reflection allows you to deepen your appreciation for the positive aspects of your life and helps you focus on the reasons behind your gratitude.

4. How It Made Me Feel: Describe the emotions or sensations you experienced when reflecting on the things you are grateful for. Acknowledging your feelings can enhance your awareness of the positive impact gratitude has on your well-being.

5. Affirmation or Intention: Conclude your gratitude journal entry by setting a positive affirmation or intention for the day ahead. This could be a statement of gratitude, a goal you want to focus on, or a reminder to maintain a positive mindset.

6. Bonus: Optional Prompts or Reflections: You can include additional prompts or reflections in your gratitude journal to further enhance your practice. This could involve writing about a specific person you are grateful for, a challenging situation that taught you valuable lessons, or a moment of personal growth and resilience.

Tips for Maintaining a Gratitude Journal:

- **Make it a Daily Habit:** Set aside a few minutes each day to write in your gratitude journal. Consistency is key to reaping the benefits of gratitude practice.

- **Be Specific and Genuine:** Focus on specific details when expressing gratitude rather than generic statements. Authenticity in your gratitude reflections can amplify the positive emotions associated with gratitude.

- **Mix It Up:** Experiment with different formats or prompts to keep your gratitude practice engaging and varied. You can incorporate drawings, quotes, or photos to personalize your journal entries.

- **Reflect on Challenges:** Embrace the opportunity to find gratitude in difficult or challenging situations. Reflecting on setbacks with a grateful mindset can foster resilience and growth.

- **Share Your Gratitude:** Consider sharing your gratitude journal entries with a trusted friend or loved one. Sharing gratitude can deepen connections and inspire others to cultivate their own practice.

By incorporating a gratitude journal template into your daily routine, you can enhance your emotional well-being, shift your perspective towards positivity, and foster a deeper sense of happiness and contentment in your life. Remember that practicing gratitude is a journey, and each entry in your gratitude journal is a step towards embracing the abundance of positivity in your life.

Printed in Great Britain
by Amazon

45674533R00076